Progress

A Reconstruction

Peter Wagner

polity

First published in 2016 by Polity Press

Polity Press
65 Bridge Street
Cambridge CB2 1UR, UK

Polity Press
350 Main Street
Malden, MA 02148, USA

ISBN-13: 978-0-7456-9099-5
ISBN-13: 978-0-7456-9100-8(pb)

A catalogue record for this book is available from the British Library.

Library of Congress Cataloging-in-Publication Data

Wagner, Peter, 1956 September 18–
    Progress: a reconstruction / Peter Wagner.
      pages cm
    Includes bibliographical references and index.
    ISBN 978-0-7456-9099-5 (hardback: alk. paper) – ISBN 978-0-7456-9100-8
(pbk.: alk. paper)   1. Progress.   2. Social change.   I. Title.
    HM891.W34 2015
    303.4–dc23
                  2015017032

Typeset in 11 on 14 pt Sabon
by Toppan Best-set Premedia Limited
Printed and bound in the UK by CPI Group (UK) Ltd, Croydon, CRO 4YY

For further information on Polity, visit our website: politybooks.com

Contents

Foreword

In 1799, a decade after the French Revolution and the death of the enlightened monarch Carlos III, Francisco de Goya etched *El sueño de la razon produce monstruos*, reproduced on the cover of this book, as a part of his series *Los caprichos*. The etching can be interpreted as a commitment to the Enlightenment belief in reason: when reason sleeps, monsters will take over. But it can also be read more ambivalently: it is the dream of reason to create monsters that will rule the world.

One of the dreams of Enlightenment reason was that humankind would embark on a path of perpetual progress. More than two centuries later, we are not sure what to make of this dream. If we look at the current world, can we see it as the dream come true? A world of material abundance, of widespread commitment to freedom and human rights, and in a global process of democratization? Or did reason fall into deep slumber, dreamless or nightmarish, leaving us with poverty and violence and adding the destruction of the planet to the older evils of humankind?

Not sure what to make of the dream, we have tended to forget about it. The idea of progress is out of joint with the current time. Maybe not any idea of progress, but the grand idea of historical progress, of general progress of humankind. And maybe this is as it should be. Maybe the grand idea of progress was a dreamlike projection onto future history of unrealizable wishes and desires, and by now we know that this was nothing more than a dream.

Even if this were so, this book suggests that it is worth the effort to retrieve the idea of progress, review it and see whether one can reconstruct it on new terms, appropriate for our time. The expectations of progress may have been exaggerated, but they provided human beings with an orientation in space and time. Progress had a place: it originated in Western Europe with the scientific revolution, the French Revolution, and the Industrial Revolution. And it opened up a new time, a future history with an open horizon, during which progress would spread across the whole planet. This is how West Europeans used to see world history, and this view gave them confidence about what to do and to expect.

As we shall see, this belief was often shaken, not least during the first half of the twentieth century, but it proved unwilling to die. Even in recent times, though more rarely, both public debate and academic research could refer to some countries and their people as 'advanced industrial societies' or 'advanced democracies', whereas other societies still had to 'develop', to 'catch up', or more recently, to 'emerge'. Even though philosophy of history had long been discredited as a genre, some sense still prevailed that there is a direction in which human history moves. And the predominant view was that this direction was a good one, that there had been progress and will be more progress, opposed only by those who were not ready for the new times. The starting observation of this essay is that we are losing this sense entirely – not today or yesterday, not suddenly, but gradually, starting in the past half century and more radically since the late 1970s.

This loss should be welcomed for many reasons. This view created a spatio-temporal hierarchy that denied human beings in many parts of the globe 'coevalness' with the people of the North, to paraphrase Johannes Fabian. It justified domination over human beings against their will but for the supposed benefit of humankind in the name of progress. Today, in contrast, it often seems that the farewell to a misplaced overconfidence in the spatio-temporal ordering of the globe has been replaced by generalized disorientation. And this is neither necessary nor desirable.

Is there a place between the overconfidence of the past and the disorientation of the present? If we abandon the dream of perpetual progress, is there a way of going on that still means going forward? Are there ways to reconsider the doubts about progress without leaving us with nothing but doubts?

These questions are interesting, some readers may now say, but can we really answer them? After all, there were good reasons why philosophy of history was abandoned. And that kind of historical sociology that sweepingly talked about long-lasting trends and great ruptures, which emerged during the nineteenth century in the wake of philosophy of history, was exposed to similar criticism with the professionalization and the specialization of the social sciences during the twentieth century. Maybe we should be content with the kind of knowledge that solid empirical research can provide and stop asking questions that we cannot answer.

This essay proceeds on the assumption that we should at least try. The questions are too important to be left without answers – or, maybe worse, to be left with the numerous inadequate answers that are currently given. The questions that were posed by the best of historical sociology remain alive and urgent, but they need to be addressed by new means. (The bibliographical note at the end of this book hints at what those means are and where they can be found.

Readers with methodological interest may want to read this note first.)

But what exactly can we expect from this attempt? The answer is simple: to avoid having to accept the present time as it is. Our present time is the realization of some of many possibilities created in the past. An exploration of our place in time helps us to understand the range of past possibilities and the reasons why many of them were discarded and few of them realized. Situating the present in time, thus, is a way of comparing the real with the possible. From this angle, the possible always has two forms: the past possible and the present possible. Historical sociology helps us to understand the possibilities of the past, the struggle over which has created the present. To analyse these struggles from the angle of the claims for the future that were then made, in turn, helps us to see the present as providing a range of possibilities for our future. In this sense, there is a direction of history that no quarrel over method or dissection of concepts will make disappear. But we cannot advance in this direction on a road already laid out; we need to go ahead by building the road where we want it to lead. The purpose of this essay is to explore past possibilities with a view to better understanding present possibilities. If it succeeds, some sense of orientation will be restored, hopefully an adequate sense.

I am very grateful to Laurent Jeanpierre, who suggested to me that I write this book and offered the possibility of publishing it in the series *L'Horizon des possibles*, which he co-directs with Christian Laval at *La Découverte*. Without his suggestion, it would never have been written in this form. The idea was subsequently picked up for the English edition by John Thompson at Polity, whom I would like to thank for his continued interest in my work and his support.

The research on which this work is based has received generous support from the European Research Council for the project 'Trajectories of modernity: comparing non-European and European varieties' (TRAMOD), funded as Advanced Grant no. 249438. Most significantly, the grant made it possible to create the TRAMOD research group, which has provided a place for exploration, inspiration and critique over the past five years. I would like to thank all members of the group for extended discussions of the main ideas of this essay, as well as of fragments of the text on various occasions. Special thanks go to Angela Lorena Fuster Peiró, Nathalie Karagiannis, Aurea Mota and Gerard Rosich who read the whole or parts of the manuscript and provided detailed comments. Johann Arnason and Gerard Delanty offered encouragement in the early stages of the writing. The main outlines of the reasoning were presented in lectures at Ural Federal University, Ekaterinburg, in April 2014 and at the Centre de Cultura Contemporània de Barcelona in March 2015. Intense exchanges with Axel Honneth and Luc Boltanski about the relation between their perspectives and mine allowed further refinement of the ideas. I am also grateful to two anonymous readers for Polity Press for their careful reading and their suggestions.

Barcelona, 23 April 2015

1

The Withering Away of Progress

Something Happened Between 1979 and 1989

Between 1979 and 1989, the world changed. But we have as
yet failed to understand precisely what happened and how
and, even much less so, why. The year 1979 is that of the
second oil-price hike, of the Iranian Revolution, of the election of Margaret Thatcher as prime minister of the United
Kingdom, and of the publication of Jean-François Lyotard's
Condition postmoderne. The year 1989 is that of the fall of
the Berlin Wall, during which political scientist Francis
Fukuyama declared 'the end of history' and philosopher
Richard Rorty put his suggestion between book covers
(1989) that social and political thought may already have
had 'the last conceptual revolution it needs'. Lyotard claimed
that societies are not as intelligible as social and political
thought had assumed and were far from embarked on a
historical trajectory of linear evolution. Iran, in turn, had
long been seen as being on a stable course of 'modernization
and development', but the overthrow of the Shah regime
demonstrated that other avenues are possible. Ten years
later, the beginning of the end of Soviet-style socialism, in

contrast, seemed to confirm the view that 'there is no alter-native', to paraphrase Margaret Thatcher, to market capital-ism and liberal democracy. In their characteristically different ways, Fukuyama and Rorty assessed and welcomed this new situation in society and politics, as well as in intellectual life.

Despite their all-too-evident flaws, Lyotard's, Fukuyama's and Rorty's ideas captured an important aspect of their time. We may call this aspect *the end of progress*. On the face of it, Lyotard suggested that progress was not – or no longer – possible, whereas Fukuyama and Rorty claimed that all significant progress had already been achieved. The upshot, though, is the same: if the diagnosis is correct, progress is no longer possible in our time. Even the relentless theoretical optimist Jürgen Habermas (1990) declared his adherence to the spirit of the time by calling the end of Soviet socialism a 'catching-up revolution'. Like the hare in the tale, 'progres-sive' political activists around the world found themselves at the end of their race looking at the liberal-democrat hedge-hog who smilingly says 'I am already here'.

But now it seems that, like the hedgehog couple,[1] liberal-democratic philosophy of history has played a mirror trick on humankind. Upon arrival, the final destination of the journey did not at all correspond with the image that had been used in the publicity. From the 1990s onwards, unbound capitalism has led to an increase in inequality, a worsening of working conditions and the dismantling of the welfare state where it existed. There are now large areas on the earth where lawfulness no longer exists and violence appears to be ever more widespread. Furthermore, the ecology of the planet is ever more unbalanced, moving us rapidly closer to the moment in which living conditions will dramatically

---

[1]To recall the Grimm brothers' tale: The hedgehog challenged the hare to run a race. And he 'won' it without running by placing his wife, indistinguishable from him, at the end of the course.

deteriorate due to climate change. All we can expect, therefore, seems to be a continuation of wars and violence, poverty
and inequality, exploitation and oppression, interrupted
only, at best, by spatially and temporally limited periods in
which relative peace, well-being, equality and freedom can
be obtained. The optimism of those who thought that the
promise of progress has already been fulfilled has yielded to
the pessimism of those who think that lasting progress is
unachievable. The only possible meaning of progress in our
time, as Claus Offe recently suggested, is the avoidance of
regress. And we will have to work hard even to achieve this.

Later on, we will need to paint a more nuanced picture
of the present. After all, we also live at a time in which a
considerable increase in material wealth is created in the so-
called 'emerging economies'. Transformation-oriented governments in Latin America and South Africa have achieved
significant reduction in poverty and increase in welfare provision. Arguably, there are fewer oppressive regimes now
than there were fifty years ago. Apartheid in South Africa
and military dictatorships in Latin America have been overcome and have in some places given way to vibrant participa-
tory democracy. Maybe hopes for progress have only been
abandoned in that region of the earth where such radical
hopes were generated in the first place – the north-west –
whereas they are flourishing elsewhere.

Let us, however, postpone the more detailed look at current
reality and try first to understand the (partial) disillusionment about the present in the light of prior expectations.
Disillusionment, after all, can be a positive process. It means
liberation from unfounded illusions. Maybe something had
been wrong with progress to start with. The world we live
in today may be the result of us humans trying to bring into
being a world that cannot – or should not – exist. Or of us
trying to create such a world by the wrong means, by means
through which it cannot – or should not – be created. The

point here is not only that our view of that better future world or of the ways in which it can be brought about was possibly flawed. The point also is that the fact of us having tried has indeed transformed the world, and not – or not only – for the better. Thus I suggest that we review the history of the idea of progress and the way it has helped to transform the world to understand our present condition and our present malaise.

Some readers may now think that this is typical conservative reasoning. I want to ask them for a bit of patience; I will explicitly address conservatism later on. It is not my purpose to discard the commitment to progress altogether by showing how the pursuit of progress made the world a worse place to live in. And this for two reasons: firstly, because this is not true. The pursuit of progress made the world both better and worse, at different times, in different places and in different respects. We have to understand the reasons for these variations. And, secondly, because it is exactly our dissatisfaction with the present state of the world that requires us to continue exploring possibilities for progress. If there were flaws in the past conception of progress, leading to negative consequences in its application, then we need to see whether we can remedy both the conceptual flaws and the negative consequences by elaborating and using a more adequate notion of progress. That is why we first need to see how the concept of progress emerged that guided much of human action over two centuries.

A Look Back: The Invention of Progress

In the most general sense, progress means improvement in the living conditions of human beings, not least in their ways of living together. Progress is always temporal; it refers to improvement through a comparison over time. In this general sense, to the best of our knowledge human beings have always been concerned with progress. They have seen it happening and have reflected on the reasons for it, not least on the conditions for bringing it about. They have also witnessed decline and have reflected on possibilities of avoiding it. Observing their past, they have sometimes made distinctions between improvements in some respects and decline in others. Mostly, they have not expected improvements to be lasting accomplishments. Everything that could improve could also deteriorate again, and was likely to do so at some point.

However, something very particular occurred in Europe during the seventeenth and eighteenth centuries. The expectation arose that comprehensive improvement was possible, improvement in all respects. And such improvement would not necessarily be only temporary. It could be sustained in the long run, and every future situation could be subject to further improvement. Furthermore, such comprehensive improvement was not only possible; it was even likely to happen because one had gained insight into the conditions needed for it to emerge. This change of expectations was the *invention of progress*. As we shall see, it is these events to which those of the present provide the mirror. They mark the moment when the race between hare and hedgehog started. We will not be able to run it again but, in order to understand where we are now, we have to review its course.

By 1800, the reinterpretation of the idea of progress had such pronounced effects that historians have spoken of a 'rupture in societal consciousness' (Koselleck and Reichardt 1988), more precisely associated with the French Revolution as the moment of breakthrough of the new concept. In possibly the most striking formulation, Reinhart Koselleck has captured the emergence of the new idea of progress as the separation of the horizon of expectations from the space of experience, thus as the wide opening of the horizon of time. That which was possible in the future was no longer determined by the experiences of the past.

Two aspects of the then emerging concept of progress are particularly important for our work at reconstruction. First, the separation of expectations from experiences created a wide gap between the past and the future. Progress is that which takes place in this gap. Progress is a linear path that leads from the limited past experiences to an ever better future. Thus an asymmetry is created between improvement and deterioration, between progress and regress. While the latter cannot be entirely ruled out, it is temporary and no more than the result of obstacles to be overcome in the course of progress. Furthermore, progress is in principle endless: it does not lead to an end state, to perfection; rather, human history is characterized by ever further perfectability. Progress is a processual term. Koselleck calls this aspect 'temporalization', and he uses the term 'horizon' to express the absence of an end-point that can be reached.

Secondly, rather than referring to 'forward moves' (progress; *Fort-schritt*) in this or that respect, thus in the plural, progress becomes a 'collective singular' (Koselleck 2006) as a comprehensive term for appreciating the sum of numerous phenomena. Now one could speak of 'progress of humankind', uniting the destiny of all human beings, and of 'progress of history', which is the process that fills the gap between past and future. Between these two terms, furthermore, there is an important shift of emphasis. When humanity progresses, it can be seen as both the subject of progress, those who are doing the progressing, and as the object, those with and for whom progress takes place. When history progresses, the subject is not evidently any human agent any longer. In the course of the nineteenth century, progress becomes ever more something that happens on its own and towards which human beings have to position themselves. One can be on the side of progress, and one can fail to be so, with significant consequences.

In comparison with any view of improvement held before, the new concept of progress marked a radical break. It connected normative advances in the human condition with a long and linear perspective. And it disconnected those advances from direct human agency; progress itself came to be endowed with causal agency. We can call this a *strong concept of progress*. It envisaged a positive transformation in the human condition of a radical kind that had never been considered as even remotely possible before. Doing so, it detached the normative expectations regarding the future from the current evidence about social life in Europe – the place where this concept emerged – during the eighteenth and nineteenth centuries.

Put in these terms, one immediately recognizes our current distance from this conception of progress. We are not inclined to hold this strong belief any longer. Our doubts concern both the underlying philosophy of history, with its normative-evolutionist thrust, and the 'method', namely the detaching of expectations from experiences. We may even show some incredulity that such beliefs could reasonably have been held at other times. Turning things around, it is precisely to better understand our experiences with progress that we need to inquire into the assumptions on which this concept of progress was built.

This inquiry, to be pursued in more detail later, quickly yields a first and very general result. Those whom we call Enlightenment thinkers shared one basic assumption on which everything else was built: they saw human beings as capable of autonomy and as endowed with reason.[2] Reason

---

[2]If one adopted Kant's distinction between reason and understanding, then the term 'understanding' would be more appropriate here. In general usage, however, the term 'reason' is more common and the distinction is rarely made.

allowed them the insight into the problems they were facing and the development of the means to solve them. Autonomy allowed them to choose the adequate means and to take the appropriate action. This is what enables improvement in terms of solving problems. Furthermore, human beings have memory and can learn. Therefore, rather than every generation having to address the same problem again, successive generations can build on the achievements of the earlier ones and improve on them. This connection of reason, autonomy and learning capacity is what creates the conditions for the historical progress of humankind.

If this is so, however, one further question immediately arises, namely the question of why there has not been more and more sustained progress in human history up to 1800. But the question, too, found a plausible answer at the time. Humankind then stood only at the 'exit from self-incurred immaturity' (Immanuel Kant). It had not yet dared to make full use of its capacity to reason; and often enough human beings had not been free, not autonomous; they were living under various forms of domination. But this was about to change, not least as a consequence of Enlightenment thought, so one assumed. And once the conditions for human beings to live autonomously and to reason freely were created, then progress would impose itself and could no longer be stopped. With this additional insight, we not only understand why there has not been that much progress before 1800; we are furthermore given reasons why expectations about future progress under conditions of autonomy should detach themselves from the past experiences made under conditions of 'immaturity'.

The two preceding paragraphs are a caricature of Enlightenment thought. Hardly any thinker can be found who endorses this reasoning in such a simplistic way. But a caricature exaggerates features that are indeed there, and so does this. In other words, without maintaining some commitment to the beneficial combination of freedom and reason, it would have been impossible to arrive at the strong notion of progress described above, and to display the optimism that goes along with it.

The Experience with Progress: A Note on Method

After these reflections, it may seem clear what we have to do. We should review the historical experiences with progress since the inauguration of the strong concept and assess how far they match the expectations to which this concept had given rise when it was coined: a history of progress from, let's say, 1789 to 1989, to make things simple. But, arguably, this review has already been done and has led to the outcome mentioned at the outset. The concept of progress has withered away because it exhausted itself. Critical thinkers, furthermore, often hold the view that this exhaustion signals failure. A friend with whom I talked about the ideas for this book asked whether I had not considered calling it *Progress Remembered* or *Progress in Retrospect*. He assumed that any such exercise could only be 'historical' in the sense that it will demonstrate that no idea of progress can be upheld in the present. And a reviewer of the book proposal said he or she had just read Thomas Piketty's *Capital in the Twenty-First Century* (2013) and concluded that there was no point in the proposed exercise of reconstructing the idea of progress in the face of the evidence of ineradicable structures of inequality – in other words, that history had already shown that progress was not possible. Other observers are more complacent. They do not necessarily assume that everything is good as it is, but they do hold that further intellectual or institutional innovations that could bring future progress are not envisageable any more. Exhaustion has here a more benign meaning, but it spells the end to progress nevertheless. Thus all we can do with progress is look nostalgically back at it. Nostalgically, since we know we can never go back home because home is not in another place, it was at another time.

The following reflections are guided by a different view. True, we have reason to believe that the history of the two centuries between 1789 and 1989 was shaped by expectations of progress. We may even say that the belief in possible progress had a transformative power on human beings, social life and the earth – these transformations will be sketched in subsequent chapters. But this does not mean that those two centuries should be interpreted as the realization of this concept so that everything significant that happened, for better or worse, can be related to, or even explained by, the work of this concept. The relation between concepts and history is more complicated than this. I have to briefly explain how I am going to address it.

Human beings are 'self-interpreting animals' (Charles Taylor). The ways in which they interpret the world has a shaping impact on the world. But interpretative devices such as socio-political concepts are not of the kind that can be 'realized' in the form of a straightforward transfer into a practice or an institution. In turn, practices and institutions may well be informed by concepts, even created and sustained by them, and as such they should be analysed. But they are not the unequivocal realization of any concept. One can say, to give an example, that the concept of liberty informed many institutional innovations in post-revolutionary France. But it would be wrong to say that the concept of liberty was realized in the institutions of post-revolutionary France.

The main reason why this is so resides in the inherent ambivalence of many socio-political concepts. Philosophers referred to such concepts as 'essentially contested' (W. B. Gallie), but we do not need to retrieve the whole debate that this term triggered. The key point is that concepts show an openness to interpretation and, more specifically, that there is a requirement for particular interpretation once a concept is to be 'applied' in practice. To continue the above example, post-revolutionary France witnessed the application of a concept of liberty that was unequal – it did not give the same rights of freedom to everyone – and favoured certain freedoms over others – the freedom of commerce over the freedom of association, to mention just one aspect.

This openness to interpretation becomes further significant in the face of the recalcitrance of the world when submitted to the application of concepts. During the first half of the nineteenth century, undesired consequences of the specific application of the concept of liberty were recognized, and movements for reinterpretation began that insisted on equal freedom and on the necessity for flanking the concept of liberty with that of solidarity. In other words, the experience with the application of a specific concept leads to processes of reinterpretation. Socio-political change is not least based on conceptual reinterpretation.

These reflections guide the approach that will be taken in what follows. 'Essentially contested concepts' are most often comprehensive evaluative concepts. This is certainly true for the strong concept of progress we identified above: progress was supposed to occur for human life in general and across history, and progress was seen as good. If we now consider that this comprehensive evaluative concept cannot be realized as such, we can no longer see the two centuries after 1789 as *the* historical experience with progress. Rather, we need to investigate how the concept of progress was interpreted and how its specific interpretations were applied to different walks of life. Over such a long period, furthermore, we should be able to identify specific experiences with progress that led to reinterpretations of the concept.

Anticipating the interim outcome, this approach will make it possible to see the alleged exhaustion of progress in the late twentieth century as pointing to the need for radically reinterpreting the concept for our time. This objective of reinterpretation will be pursued in the second part of this essay. There is no need for nostalgia. Instead, a sober look back will provide the conditions for a constructive look forward.

Dimensions of Progress

Is it conceivable to have made progress in some respects, but to have regressed in others? Can one develop criteria to assess whether progress has been achieved? Are there even ways of measuring (some dimensions of) progress? These were questions which worried the Académie de Dijon in 1750 when it issued an essay competition on the question: 'Has the restoration of the sciences and the arts contributed to refining moral practices?' The award-winning essay was handed in by Jean-Jacques Rousseau, who suggested that scientific progress had gone along with moral regress. His negative answer inaugurated a long-lasting tradition of thinking about the relation between scientific-technical progress and moral-cultural decline. Theodor W. Adorno and Max Horkheimer's *Dialectic of Enlightenment* can be read as using the figure of speech that Rousseau had introduced.

But there are also historico-sociologically more specific examples. Before the subjection of Europe to Nazism, European observers had often looked at the United States as an image of their own future, as a form of modernity that had progressed beyond their own. The wish to evaluate those two different interpretations of modernity and position oneself towards them led to distinctions between dimensions: most observers were struck by, and often abhorred, techno-economic progress in the United States: the conveyor belts in the Detroit car factories and the industrialized killing in the Chicago slaughterhouses were the most cited examples. Socio-political progress was identified with democracy and greater equality, not least between women and men, and it, too, was viewed ambivalently, depending on the standpoint of the observer – praised by visiting trade unionists but condemned by more aristocratically minded Europeans. In combination, finally, many observers were sceptical in moral-philosophical terms: they saw a way of life that entailed standardization and conformism and spelt an end to ideas of self-realization that were prevalent among the European upper classes. During the nineteenth century, similarly, 'modernizers' in societies outside or on the fringes of Europe had often operated distinctions between the positive elements that one should take from the supposedly more advanced societies and the problematic ones that one should – and, as the assumption often was, could – avoid. Thus distinctions within the concept of progress were introduced.

Following the agenda of disentangling an overly comprehensive concept, a distinction of dimensions of progress will be elaborated upon in what follows, and the ways in which progress can be assessed along those dimensions will be explored. For each dimension, I will first discuss how progress was envisaged, or whether it was envisaged at all. Subsequently, I will review – in all due brevity – the historical experiences with progress on each dimension, as well as the interpretations of those experiences. Finally, I will ask what needs to be rethought about progress on the respective dimension.

What are the most significant dimensions of progress? All societies have to provide answers to some core concerns when living together. Most centrally, they have to answer the questions: how are the material needs of the members of society satisfied; what are the rules for living together and how are they determined; what are the knowledge resources that our life in common can rely on? These questions refer to what can be called the basic problematics of human social life – the economic, the political and the epistemic *problématique*. Different societies have answered – and still answer – these questions in different ways. Different answers may have some degree of incommensurability between them. They cannot necessarily be compared in strictly performative terms. Nevertheless, one can pose the question whether some societies are more 'successful' (Hall and Lamont 2009) than others in answering them; or whether some answers – in general, or in given contexts – are better than others. This opens the path for an investigation of progress. Thus, in the following I will explore views of progress, criteria for progress and experiences with progress with regard to *economic progress, political progress* and *epistemic progress*.

Arguably, though, something is missing from this list. Emerging from the debates about equal freedom and solidarity, as mentioned above, critical thought focused on issues such as alienation, anomie and conformism that do not fall clearly into any of the three preceding categories. Rather than addressing problems, these issues raise a different concern, one about social conditions for self-realization. From at least the middle of the nineteenth century onwards, these issues were explored in analysis and subjected to criticism in the form of the then emerging social sciences. An underlying idea was that the ongoing socio-political transformations, which were widely hailed as progressive because of 'functional' improvements in addressing one or more of the three basic *problématiques*, had been accompanied by a decline in the possibilities for self-realization. This issue could not easily be dealt with because, in the view of many observers, it was characteristic of the new society – the inadvertent result of the apparently progressive transformation into a society based on freedom and reason. As we shall see later in detail (chapter 3), such a diagnosis gave rise to what we have come to know as critical social theory. A comprehensive criticism was provided that, initially, postulated the need for a further radical social transformation as a condition for progress and, when such transformation failed to materialize, tended to abandon hope of progress entirely. In contrast to either of these attitudes, I will suggest that it is possible, even though more difficult, to identify a specific form of progress related to this issue. Improvements in the general conditions for self-realization are what this progress, here to be called *social progress*, is about.

For clarity of exposition, the four dimensions of progress will be discussed in the order in which they – broadly – historically emerged across those two centuries under consideration: epistemic progress, economic progress, social progress and political progress. As we shall see, there are distinctions with regard to both the expectations of future progress and the assessment of accomplished progress that set the former two apart from the latter two. For this reason, epistemic and economic progress will be analysed in chapter 2, and social and political progress in chapter 3.

A Look Forward: Embarking on the Work of Reconstruction

In the course of the analysis of the dimensions of progress, as undertaken in chapters 2 and 3, we shall see that the respective understandings of progress all refer to the underlying idea of an articulation of freedom with reason that engenders irresistible progress. However, the interpretations of the component concepts – freedom and reason – vary considerably across the four dimensions, as does the way in which these two components are articulated with each other. Furthermore, the temporality of progress is important. Progress was seen as achieved along some dimensions much earlier than along others. And over time the view of how specific progress could be achieved was also subject to change. This differentiated finding suggests that we need to take a second look at how freedom and reason were seen by the Enlightenment thinkers and their followers. This will be done in chapter 4 with a view to identifying the flaws, if any, in the articulation between freedom and reason that help us to understand why the concept of progress withered away.

As a result of this work at differentiation, some features come to stand out that bring the dimensions of progress into relation with each other. In some views, epistemic and economic progress would provide the conditions for social and political progress; in others, as hinted at above, the opposite was the case. Significantly, the criteria for progress appeared much clearer and rather consensual with regard to knowledge and needs, whereas they were more contested and doubtful with regard to social and political matters. Finally, and this is a key insight, some exhaustion can be observed in western societies around 1970 in all dimensions of progress – often with the ambiguity mentioned above between exhaustion seen ultimately as failure or ultimately as success. But again, of what kind this exhaustion was and what the reasons for it were remains a matter of debate within the areas, as much as the question of whether and how the exhaustion can be overcome. What is required, therefore, as a subsequent step, is a contextual diagnosis of the current state of progress. This diagnosis will rejoin the elements of the pluridimensional analysis of progress (chapters 2 and 3) in the light of the conceptual reconsideration of the articulation between freedom and reason as a condition for progress (chapter 4). This will be done in chapter 5, which will analyse what happened to progress over the past half century.

At this point, it is useful to anticipate the steps that will be taken in chapters 4 and 5 in a nutshell. The original expectation of progress had been based on the assumption that the era of autonomy had begun and that free and reason-endowed human beings would not do other than steadily improve the condition of humankind. In historical reality, however, freedom had certainly not been achieved by all. Rather, a minority of free human beings exercised their autonomy with a view to dominating nature, others outside their own society and the unfree majority in their own society. And such domination, in turn, was increasingly resisted by this unfree majority, by the dominated others elsewhere and also by nature. Much of the progress – in the sense of transformation of the human condition – over the two centuries of the reign of the strong concept, therefore, was not due to the interaction between free human beings, but resulted from domination and the resistance to domination.[3] In some respects, such progress indeed entailed normative advances, as will be discussed in what follows. But such historically identifiable progress was not achieved on the grounds hypothesized by the advocates of the strong concept of progress. The important conclusion to be drawn from this insight, then, is that the withering away of progress in the recent past cannot be due to flaws in the Enlightenment idea of a progressive articulation of freedom and reason. That idea cannot even be said to have been refuted, as Lyotard put it. Because the conditions for its application were not fulfilled; rather, there was no way of knowing

---

[3] Some readers may see here an affinity to the reasoning proposed by critical theorists from Marx onwards, and some such affinity indeed exists. As will be shown in chapter 4, however, Marx and other critical theorists erred in following Enlightenment thinkers in the assumption that the era of full autonomy had already begun.

through experience whether it was flawed or not. In a world marked by domination, we do not know how and with which outcome human beings make use of their reason. Chapter 4 will demonstrate how critical thinkers from the late eighteenth to the early twentieth century showed awareness of this issue, but failed to address it appropriately.

In this light, those who declared the end of progress in the late twentieth century missed the point when they grasped their present as the outcome of trying to realize the strong concept of progress in history, failed or accomplished. But they were right in identifying the withering away of this strong concept of progress in their time, and for this we need an alternative interpretation. Chapter 5 will try to provide such alternative interpretation through a world-sociological analysis of the socio-political transformation that started with the acceleration of decolonization in 1960; proceeded with the varieties of '1968' rebellions across large parts of the world; turned towards economic 'adjustments' that entailed major relocation of world production, loss of state control over the economy and the weakening of the force of labour; and culminated in the fall of Soviet socialism and in an era during which 'globalization' and 'individualization' became catchwords that stood for an adequate understanding of the time. It is easy to see that high hopes for progress were raised during the 1960s to then collapse, like the energy explosion of dying stars, within a very few years. It is more difficult to understand exactly what happened.

Without anticipating the detail of the analysis, I want to propose seeing what happened as the (near) end of formal domination. This may sound like a version of the 'end of history' thesis, but it is not. The end of formal domination is not the end of domination. The struggle for personal and collective self-determination continues. But it changes form, and this rather radically. Formal domination shall be understood as a kind of domination that justifies hierarchy of one category of persons over another and enshrines such hierarchy in formal rules that, among other elements, determine who dominates and who is dominated. Formal domination was widespread across the globe by 1960: of colonizers over the colonized; of settlers and their descendants over indigenous populations; of men over women; of owners of capital over the owners of labour power; of the leaders of organized collectivities over the members; of the authorized interpreters of hegemonic philosophies of history over those whose expressions were censored and oppressed; of those who had the right to political participation over those who did not; among others. Today, formal domination has certainly not entirely disappeared, but it is much less widespread and much less pronounced than it was half a century ago.[4]

[4] This definition includes an element of self-understanding, that is, the way a collectivity conceives of itself, its members and the relations between them, and an element of institutionalization, that is, the codification of such self-understanding in explicit rules that are observed and enforced. Admittedly, the term 'formal domination' may be found wanting in many respects. Even beyond terminology, the definition requires refinement with a view to distinguishing as clearly as possible formal domination from other kinds of domination. But, preferably, I would like to see such refinement proceeding from an exploration of the underlying thesis, rather than from conceptual debate alone: the thesis, namely, that there has been a radical transformation in the meaning of domination over the past half century, a transformation that critical thought and public debate still need to take fully into account. Those who are reluctant to accept this thesis, to be underpinned in chapter 5, may consider it as an invitation to analyse in detail the relation between domination and autonomy and its historical transformations.

And this is the main reason for the withering away of progress as traditionally understood. Rather than the outcome of the exercise of autonomy, progress for two centuries was the combined outcome of the exercise of domination and the resistance to domination. We still have to take full account of the transformation of the world as the result of this progress – and whether and in which respect we want to call this result progress. But if we live at the end of formal domination, then there is also another task that we have to accomplish: we have to rethink possible progress after the end of formal domination.

This is a difficult task because the required change of perspective is radical. Whenever it maintained the hope of progress, critical thought tended to equate significant progress with the end of domination. For this reason, little intellectual energy was spent on considering what kind of progress would be possible and necessary after the end of domination. Inadvertently, there was a displaced return to Enlightenment optimism, assuming that freedom and reason would easily go hand in hand once domination was overcome. Now that formal domination is largely overcome but problems are overwhelming, things often turn to the worse and progress fails to materialize, critical thought is at a loss. Reasoning that suggests that formal domination persists and keeps standing in the way of progress is not entirely wrong, obviously not. But it diverts energy from the more urgent task: considering precisely how the interaction of autonomous human beings, capable of understanding, can bring about progress in the most pressing concerns of our time. Because this is the condition of our time, for the first time in human history. And we keep failing to address it. We keep considering our failure to achieve progress as being due to formal domination that prevents us from doing what needs to be done. We rarely suppose that thinking and acting together in the appropriate way is a problem in its own right, not the fault of someone or something else. The remainders of formal domination serve as an excuse for not exploring the conditions for, and maybe also limitations to, achieving progress through autonomy.

The concluding chapter 6 will address this task, but not much needs to be said about it at this point. In conceptual terms, I will propose to replace the strong concept of progress as an almost self-propelled force of history with a notion that focuses on agency, imagination and critique. In contextual terms, I will try to apply such a notion to the situation of our time. After first identifying different types of progress at stake today, I will propose that *one* key concern of our time should be political progress. Politics need to be understood today in terms of a radical commitment to democratic agency, giving different meaning to the widely used concept of 'democratization', which in practice often entails a decreasing capacity to act politically. The daunting task is, at the same time, to reverse the recent decline of state-based political capacity, create political capacity in global coordination and do so in unprecedented forms of democratic agency. The building of such democratic collective agency needs to go along with the definition of the central problems that such agency should address. That is why the *other* key concern of our time should be progress towards a more adequate interpretation of the world we live in. Such progress can only be achieved in struggle against those who have an interest in promoting world-interpretations that leave their privileges intact. After the end of formal domination, current work at world-interpretation needs to focus on the identification of new forms of domination. And it needs to combat the hubristic inclination of considering human beings as actually capable of mastering all aspects of their existence on this earth. Elaborating such a notion of progress for our time, therefore, will invite us to rethink the relation between our space of experience and our horizon of expectations.

2

Progress as Mechanism: The Epistemic-Economic Complex

Progress of Knowledge: Science, the Endless Frontier?

Progress of knowledge was constitutive of the high expectations for progress as they arose during the eighteenth century. The original notion of strong progress indeed starts out from epistemic progress, namely progress in the knowledge of nature as it had been achieved in what came to be called the scientific revolution during the sixteenth and seventeenth centuries. The term 'scientific revolution', which was coined in the early twentieth century, but the meaning of which gradually emerged from the eighteenth century onwards, refers to a profound change in the view of nature from Copernicus's heliocentric world-view to Newton's insights about gravity. There has been extended historiographical debate about the timing and even the existence of such a radical shift. Criticizing the idea of radical change, it has been suggested that there was much more continuity and rather gradual change from the thirteenth century onwards; that the early modern views reconnected to views already held in antiquity, rather than providing radical novelty; and that the European scholars who provided the new insights were drawing on numerous extra-European sources. For our purposes, it is only important to note that what was perceived was a radical change in the mode of knowledge generation and in the kind of knowledge produced.

The core observation that should underpin the strong concept of progress was that knowledge of nature can be accumulated so that future generations have superior insights. It was clearly expressed by Isaac Newton who attributed his ability to arrive at new knowledge metaphorically to his 'standing on the shoulders of giants'. Propositions of scientific knowledge might be wrong, but in that case further research and scholarly exchange would 'falsify' those propositions and they would be discarded from the stock of established knowledge, as Karl Popper would put it in the twentieth century. Such falsification meant further progress. Regress of scientific knowledge was not conceivable: once available, valid knowledge would not be forgotten. Furthermore, it appeared to contemporary observers that progress of knowledge accelerated when politico-religious restrictions on the investigation into the laws of nature were removed. Further elaborated in later debate, the idea that autonomy is the condition – or at least, one of the key conditions – for progress is already prepared in the interpretation of scientific progress.

Developments during the nineteenth century appeared to follow this interpretation. Scientific inquiry was set on new institutional foundations by the 'rise of the research-oriented university' (Wittrock 1985), in which the transfer of existing knowledge to the next generation was combined with the production of new knowledge through systematic research. More specifically, the scientific discipline provided the framework within which substantive progress of knowledge would occur. Created for the natural sciences during the early nineteenth century and for the social sciences at the turn of the nineteenth to the twentieth century, the discipline defined the substantive area of research, debated methodologies for acquiring new knowledge and created associations and journals as the sites where new knowledge was exchanged. The concept at work here was one of collective autonomy: progress of knowledge would occur when knowledge seekers communicate freely about their insights into the workings of nature – and increasingly about human beings and social life as well. The very idea of objectivity of scientific knowledge emerged when scholarly communities became so large that personal trust and direct exchange were no longer available in the degree necessary to judge the significance and accuracy of findings. They were to be replaced by methodological fiat and confirmation in replication.

While the basic idea of progress of knowledge through accumulation remained accepted, the guiding ideas as to how such accumulation should be brought about started to change in the early twentieth century for two main reasons. First, experimental research in the natural sciences required more and more equipment and laboratories that could not easily be integrated into the organizational forms of universities or academic societies. Separate institutes devoted to pursuing particular lines of research were increasingly created, an early example being the Institut Pasteur inaugurated in 1888. Secondly, research in some areas of physics and chemistry, in particular, proved to be of direct usefulness for industrial application, both for improving production technology and for the development of new consumption items such as household appliances. Thus industrial companies developed a direct interest in frontline research and started funding research in selected areas, as well as organizing their own research laboratories. The two world wars also saw the state increasingly involved in the generation of knowledge that was useful for the war effort, be it in direct military terms or in terms of sustaining an economy that had to adapt to wartime conditions.

In this context, namely when the idea of scholarly autonomy is partly replaced by the political and economic steering
of knowledge production, a critique of the sciences arises,
but significantly it is at this moment predominantly a critique
of the use of scientific knowledge, namely in the interests of
the elites or of capitalism but not of society as a whole. The
nature of scientific knowledge as progressive in terms of
increasing insight into nature and as potentially leading to
the progress of humankind, if put to good use, was hardly
questioned.

The July 1945 report to the US president, *Science: The
Endless Frontier*, signed by Vannevar Bush, a member of
the influential Bush family, is a telling document. Using the
frontier myth as the supposed evolutionary principle of US
society, but hinting at the moment when the socio-geograph-
ical significance of the frontier might exhaust itself, Bush
underlined that infinite progress was possible in science, and
that the application of scientific knowledge in society would
create the possibility of the equally infinite progress of
humanity. The report was centrally devoted to exploring
how the wartime concentration of scientific research – with
the Manhattan Project, the development of the atomic bomb,
as its most visible result – could be transformed into an
equally successful application of science to address problems
of all kinds in society, most notably health and employment.
It emphasized the continued significance of state support for
science.

The post-war period up to the 1960s and early 1970s was
generally marked by great enthusiasm about scientific
progress and its usefulness for society. The reasoning proceeded along similar lines. A French research administrator
talked about the 'closing of the last knowledge gaps' (Fraisse
1981). German social-democrats underlined how progress in
science and technology could provide economies whose
natural resources were scarce with a lasting comparative

advantage (Hauff and Scharpf 1975). This involved increasing the steering of scientific research by political actors towards areas defined as central for the economy and society. There are echoes of these debates in the current attempts at creating a 'knowledge society'.

But the 1960s also marked a turning point. Within scholarly debates, Thomas Kuhn's 1962 book, *The Structure of Scientific Revolutions*, itself provoked a revolution in the way of seeing scientific change. Kuhn suggested that major moments of change in scientific research did not occur by demonstrating that the existing knowledge was wrong or could be improved upon, but were determined by other 'extra-scientific' occurrences. This meant that the history of science could no longer be written as a history of steady progress. The book was widely debated in the theory of science. Furthermore, it triggered intense research in the history and sociology of the sciences to better understand the decisions that scientists take when they are confronted with problems of theory, methodology or interpretation of findings.

This new debate on science also reconnected with philosophical investigations about knowledge forms as they were led in the early twentieth century and found expression also in the strong critique of science as promoting objectivist, instrumentalist knowledge, such as in Theodor W. Adorno and Max Horkheimer's *Dialectic of Enlightenment*. Comparison of forms of knowledge was also undertaken in Jürgen Habermas's exploration of knowledge-guiding interests, in Cornelius Castoriadis's critique of identitarian-ensemblist logic, and Boaventura de Sousa Santos's distinction between knowledge for emancipation and knowledge for domination, among others.

If there is an outcome to those debates, it does not simply suggest that there is no progress in science. Within clearly set parameters of 'normal science' (Kuhn) or 'research programmes' (Imre Lakatos), progress can both be defined and identified. Rather, the debate suggests that different forms of knowledge can be produced by different 'approaches' or by different disciplines within the sciences addressing what appears to be the 'same' phenomenon. This difference often cannot be assessed in terms of superiority of one understanding over another. The key question then is the one about the relation between different forms of scientific knowledge. Furthermore, the debate also reintroduces the notion that science produces one kind of knowledge among others, not necessarily a superior one, and that the more interesting question today is often the one about the relation between scientific knowledge and other forms of knowledge.

At this point, therefore, one recognizes that the historically dominant perception of science as progressive was problematically equated with the notion that knowledge on which we can rely for organizing our social life is progressive. While the former may be true and may remain so in some respects and under some conditions, the latter cannot at all be taken for granted. But it is an answer to the latter question that is demanded by the epistemic *problématique*. In other words, while without doubt ever more knowledge is being produced, our societies have not provided themselves with the means to determine which knowledge should be applied to which situations.

One critical perspective on scientific progress could hold that scientific knowledge expands into areas where it does not belong; this would be an application of Habermas's notion of the colonization of the life-world to the sciences. For instance, it seems clear that progress has been made with knowledge about life extension in situations of incurable diseases, but public debate responds with concern about the right to a decent death. The question is how to relate medical-science capacities to other knowledge that human beings hold about the meaning of life and of death. Similarly, there

clearly has been long-lasting and steady progress in knowledge about extracting natural resources from the earth. But
the generation of this knowledge is driven by instrumental
interests – enhancing the profits of the extracting companies
and/or satisfying material human needs – and its application
increasingly conflicts with concerns about preserving the
inhabitability of the earth that are fed by other scientific
knowledge about earth and nature.

Economic Growth as Progress in the Satisfaction of Needs

Economic progress should be identifiable as improvement in
the satisfaction of human material needs. A useful first indicator for such satisfaction could be life expectancy. To live
presupposes that sufficient food, shelter and medical care are
available, thus that basic material needs are satisfied. Life
expectancy has varied across human history. But within the
same area, such as Europe, major historical variations can
be traced to epidemic diseases, to wars or to food shortages
due to bad harvests. Leaving out these particular situations,
life expectancy seems to have been remarkably stable. As
late as 1798, Robert Malthus suggested a basic pattern: the
tendency is for human populations to grow due to fertility.
But a moment will be reached when the available food supply
is insufficient to nourish the population. Famines, diseases
and wars have the effect of bringing population size again
to a sustainable level. Malthus did not see much possibility
of progress. But, from the late nineteenth century onwards,
life expectancy grew, first in Europe and North America,
then in many other parts of the world during the second half
of the twentieth century, from an average life expectancy of
around forty years at the beginning of the twentieth century
to more than seventy at century's end. Detailed analyses
show many of the reasons and differentiate the picture, but

for our purposes we can just conclude that with the improved supply of food, shelter and medical care, there has been significant and historically unprecedented progress in the satisfaction of material needs – over the past century and in some regions of the world.

How has this improvement in the satisfaction of material needs been achieved? To some extent this economic progress was based on epistemic progress, namely progress in the knowledge of diseases and of ways to cure or prevent them. More generally, though, this improvement was possible through the greater and more reliable provision of life-sustaining and -enhancing goods. This phenomenon has come to be called, in short, economic growth and measured as increase in the gross domestic product (GDP), a figure that became the standard indicator for improvement in living conditions by the 1960s. Postponing the critical discussion of economic growth as a measure of progress to a later moment, let me first note that this answer merely displaces the question. If economic growth brings progress, we still need to know how it is achieved. The answer to this question, in turn, is twofold. On the one hand, this progress is industrial, due to the increasing use of inanimate energy for production, thus eliminating the constraint of available wo/man power and animal power. As such, it is indeed directly related to progress of knowledge because it is the application of this latter progress in technological innovation that makes economic progress possible. There is something like an epistemic-economic complex in the debate about progress, seeing knowledge-based increases in the mastery of nature as direct causes of economic progress (I will return to this notion below). On the other hand, progress is expected from the autonomy of economic action, freeing the human 'propensity to truck, barter, and exchange one thing for another', as Adam Smith put it in *The Wealth of Nations* (1776), from the constraints imposed by feudal and mercantilist regimes and letting commerce flourish and the division of social labour increase.

Even though these two reasonings have run largely in parallel over long periods, they offer two quite distinct ways of addressing the economic *problématique*. Placing the emphasis on commerce meant expecting efficiency gains from specialization and an increasing division of labour. The trajectory of development would be one of marketization or commodification. Placing the emphasis on change in production technology due to progress of knowledge meant to expect efficiency gains from control over nature and over the production process. The trajectory would lead to increasing economies of scale and to what has been called rationalization. The one logic could be at work entirely independently of the other.[1] During the early decades of the nineteenth century, the reasoning on commercial freedom was very popular. Sometimes known as 'Smithianism', a vulgarized version of classical political economy became a public discourse used to argue for abolishing constraints and obstacles to economic action, both domestically and internationally. For this reason, Marx took this discourse as his target in his critique of political economy. But he also connected the two reasonings, suggesting that competition would lead to increasing the weight of dead over living labour and to the centralization of capital.

There is no need here to embark on a causal analysis determining whether market competition or industrialization were more important for economic growth. It seems correct to state that north-western Europe in the early nineteenth century was economically a Smithian world of trade

---

[1] Luc Boltanski and Laurent Thévenot quite appropriately made a distinction between the industrial order of worth and the market order of worth.

between relatively small-scale manufacturers. From the 1820s onwards, however, production technology started to change more rapidly. Most accounts now date the beginning of the Industrial Revolution to this moment. Whatever the predominant cause, the effects were striking. As Angus Maddison (1982) put it: 'Since 1820 the total product of the [advanced capitalist] countries considered here has increased seventy-fold, population nearly five-fold, per capita product fourteen-fold and real per capita consumption almost tenfold. Annual working hours are down by half and life expectation has doubled' (I will come back to these figures below).

As a consequence, we have become accustomed to write the history of economic progress as a sequence of industrial revolutions. The steam engine and the railways permitted the exit from Malthus's law by feeding larger populations better and avoiding the famines common to the past. This 'original' Industrial Revolution is now considered to be the first of three. In the second Industrial Revolution at the end of the nineteenth century, inventions in physics and chemistry are in the background of innovations in the electrical and chemical industry leading to life- and work-facilitating devices in the household and the firm and, thus, the emergence of consumer society, as well as establishing the preconditions for a new gender division of social labour. And most recently, the third Industrial Revolution brought the innovations in information and communications technology that made the globe shrink and provided amenities reaching from unprecedented access to information to a new and supposedly more efficient global division of social labour.

This is a picture of economic progress as a continuous process, advancing steadily, even though in technology-induced leaps. It is not an entirely incorrect picture, but if we aim to grasp historical progress in the satisfaction of material needs, it is also a very incomplete picture. To see better and more, we need to widen the perspective. Let me proceed by first appreciating the picture, something which critical observers often fail to do, then adding three observations that make its interpretation somewhat more difficult.

This picture tells us that there has been sustained progress in the satisfaction of material needs. It seems that everyone knows this, so why should we state something so obvious? The reason is that critical assessments of the history of the past two centuries have often shown a tendency to displace the discussion when faced with material human needs. Averse to admitting progress in this respect, parallel developments that can be analysed as regress have been emphasized instead. But such procedure is detrimental both to our understanding of social change and for the persuasiveness of critique. Not least because of the extraordinary dimension of change that they indicate, the few data I have presented suggest that economic progress, or at least the promise of it, may have driven much of social change over the past two centuries, even though in ways that were determined by the elites. Critics of capitalism often overlook that capitalism would probably long have ceased to exist had it not 'delivered the goods' in some, however distorted, way. Post-colonial studies have emphasized that (neo-)colonial domination placed the colonized people into an eternal 'not yet', thus conveying different speeds of progress (I return to this issue below). Significantly, however, the current forceful rejection of this 'not yet' in so-called emerging societies is often focused on reaching the same level of material progress as the 'advanced' societies, maybe even more strongly among the populations than among the elites. In a common view, this is what modernity's attraction is truly about. 'Later modernities', such as the East Asian ones, are successful precisely to the extent that they adopt western technical innovations, spread their benefits across their own societies and acquire the capacity for further technical and material progress. In turn, 'alternative modernities', such as the Soviet one or several historical attempts in Latin America, ultimately failed because they proved unable to harness material progress in the same way that the West had done. Theorists of 'neo-modernization' propagate this picture today.

But what about exploitation and alienation, critics will ask, as products of the very same process that brought economic growth about? The problem with this question is not that it is inappropriate, but that it is often asked prematurely, namely before – and de facto often instead of – having scrutinized history for material progress. The implicit assumption of critical thinking is that alienation and exploitation 'outweigh' progress in the satisfaction of needs; that is why one should concentrate on the former. But it is not at all self-evident how a comparison of these phenomena in terms of normative gains and losses should proceed. For present purposes, the practical conclusion is to temporarily separate the two phenomena. Exploitation can be understood as the refusal to participate in economic progress and will be discussed as such in a moment. Alienation can be viewed as a lack of possibilities for self-realization and will be discussed as a matter of social progress – or regress – below (in chapter 3). Taken on its own terms, then, there is no doubt that there has been material progress, and we are finally able to say so.

But the progress I have diagnosed was certainly not evenly distributed across space and time, and its diffusion was certainly not as self-propelled as the supposed alliance of science, markets and industry under the banner of autonomy and mastery suggested. The following considerations will qualify the imagery in terms of, first, the places of progress, second, the timing of progress for different social groups and, third, the dynamics of the social diffusion of progress.

1 My rough data have underlined that material progress initially took place in Europe. This phenomenon has variously been referred to as the European 'take-off' (Walt Rostow), the 'rise of Europe' or, most recently, the 'great

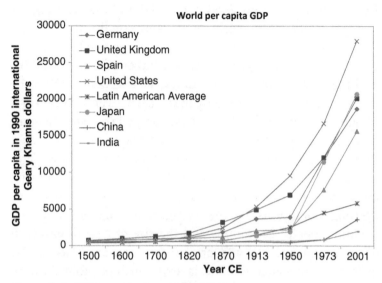

Figure 2.1 GDP per capita, 1000–1950.
Angus Maddison, The World Economy: Historical Statistics 8:
1–2001 AD, www.ggdc.net/maddison/oriindex.htm.

divergence' (Pomeranz 2000). Even with reservations about available knowledge, the figures are striking.

There is a long-lasting debate about the causes of this divergence, distinguishing between technical and socio-historical, institutional and cultural, and external and internal aspects, among other things. This debate is unlikely to ever reach a final conclusion, but one can discuss and assess the evidence that is being mobilized. In a recent and very explicit analysis, Kenneth Pomeranz suggests that, first, the – Malthusian, if one wants to put it like that – land constraint persisted in Europe as elsewhere until the early nineteenth century and, second, that it was removed for two reasons: the use of coal close to urban centres for industrial production; and the appropriation of African labour and American soil to feed and clothe the European population, thus 'freeing' it for industrial labour. This latter feature requires that

European material progress had social and material regress in other parts of the world as its likely condition.

2 Our rough data also tell us about a difference between the timing of economic growth, which 'takes off' in the 1820s, and the increase in life expectancy, which 'takes off' in the late nineteenth or mostly only in the early twentieth century. (Angus Maddison should not have lumped the two phenomena together in the above-quoted paragraph: see p. 32). And indeed descriptions of nineteenth-century Europe have deteriorating living conditions as a dominant theme: working conditions in the mines and in the industrial factories; housing conditions in the fast-growing industrial cities; declining health conditions and the rise of new diseases, to all of which one can add prostitution and crime as 'moral evils' that are related to material evils. Such phenomena were jointly addressed as 'the social question' after mid-century, and this question was often considered the key challenge that European societies had to face. In some countries, the misery led to emigration in large numbers, mostly to the Americas. Material progress, therefore, was limited to small groups in European societies during the nineteenth century, and the majority of the population either did not benefit from it – this applies to large segments of the rural population – or suffered even significant decline in their material conditions – the new industrial working class.

3 Ideologues of progress in the strong sense explained and justified such regress as a temporary phase through which societies had to pass in their unstoppable way to progress. However, there is no evidence that suggests that there has been any self-driven dynamics to leave that phase. The common view of modernity's material progress suggests, as mentioned above, that it is the combined result of the working of the technical and industrial dynamics unleashed in European history and the dynamics of market forces. We have reason to assume, though, that such dynamics on

their own would have failed to bring about the advances in living conditions that Europe had reached by, say, 1913, had not other forces been at work. The factors that were seen to bring about epistemic-economic progress could be at work while allowing the benefits to be appropriated by a small elite. This has been a common situation in most parts of the world for long periods; it remains so in many, and the situation may be about to become more generalized again. Liberal-economic thinking allows inventors and entrepreneurs to see themselves as the rightful owners of the fruits of progress. Thus, a more equal participation in material progress required action, indeed struggle, to make it happen, not least a struggle for reinterpretation. The 'social critique' (as discussed in Boltanski and Chiapello 1999) at work from the middle of the nineteenth century has been a key force that transformed a techno-economic potential into a broad societal benefit. This struggle was motivated by a sense of injustice and by the desire to improve one's living conditions on the part of social movements, most importantly the workers' movement, and by concern about the fabric and order of society on the part of the elites (Karl Polanyi's *The Great Transformation* remains a forceful analysis). And such force may accordingly be needed in the present and future as well to continue the trajectory of material progress.

By the early twentieth century, steps were being taken towards a more equal distribution of material progress through the state-centred redistribution that was the early welfare state, as well as the business-centred adjustment that became known as Fordism or consumer capitalism, in which higher wages allowed the workers to buy the products of their own work. In Continental Europe, the political terms of these changes were altered by authoritarian-totalitarian regimes and the Second World War. But after the war's end, Western Europe became both affluent and relatively egalitarian, which is a rare constellation in world history and indeed one that possibly will not last much longer.

Taking the three preceding observations together, a more elaborate, though still preliminary, picture of the dynamics of material progress emerges: material progress of unprecedented dimensions has taken place during the past two centuries of human history, but this progress was originally appropriated by small elite groups in society at the expense, indeed often the material regress, of the majority in their own society and people in other parts of the world. A temporal dimension was added to the promise of the strong concept of material progress that had emerged in the late eighteenth century: for most people in the world, this progress would happen 'not yet' but in some undefined future. This future, furthermore, was likely to remain on the distant horizon were it not for the critique that pointed to the lack of justification for the temporal inequality and for the organized protests that were based on the critique.

The Transformation of the Earth: The Emerging Great Divergence of Interpretations

Up to this point, this brief reconstruction has shown that progress of knowledge and material progress have proceeded in largely parallel ways from the late eighteenth century up to the second half of the twentieth century. The expectation of material progress as economic growth was rather closely related to the expectation of progress of knowledge because it came to be based on similar assumptions. In the second half of the eighteenth century, the connection between freedom and the increase of human capability, which supposedly had underpinned what was later called the scientific revolution, was also introduced into the debates about satisfaction of needs. Both epistemic and economic progress were, thus, particular expressions of the general linkage between freedom and reason in Enlightenment thought.

On a closer look, though, these expressions indeed showed very particular characteristics. For both epistemic and economic progress, the result of the use of reason is the increase of mastery – mastery over nature in the first instance, but mastery over human social life as well. And autonomy, rather than being a component of progress in its own right, tends to be seen as a means of achieving progress of knowledge and material progress. This similarity underlies the historically parallel development and allows us to speak of an epistemic-economic complex in the analysis of progress.

For economic progress, furthermore, the interpretation of mastery over nature and social life is purely instrumental: there is a purpose that defines the kind of mastery that is being searched for: whether this purpose is the satisfaction of material needs, economic growth or return on investment will be discussed in the following section, but there is always a purpose that guides the search for mastery. The interpretation of autonomy, in turn, is individualistic. The optimum result of market self-regulation will be reached when individual economic agents follow their own interests and communicate with others only through the mediation of prices and money.

For epistemic progress, the interpretation is more open in both these respects. In many accounts, knowledge is not sought for instrumental mastery in the first instance, but for a better understanding of the laws of nature. Practical usefulness of knowledge is often derived from such better understanding, but not seen as the immediate goal. Similarly, knowledge producers do not act on their own, individually; they communicate with others about the most significant questions to address and about the best means to answer them. The idea of autonomy that underpins epistemic progress is originally one of the autonomy of a scholarly community.

For both dimensions of progress, the interpretations of autonomy as the mechanism for generating progress supported notions of separate, self-regulating social organization of epistemic and economic practices. Later social theory turned these notions into the view of modern societies as based on functional differentiation. For our purposes, it is more important to note that this view made epistemic and economic practices exempt from social justifications – they were expected to provide maximum progress if left on their own.

This 'official', hegemonic view of the mechanisms for epistemic and economic progress still occupies a dominant position in contemporary societies. However, this view has also been subjected to critiques, the weight of which has accumulated over time. Three main such critiques can be distinguished.

First, while accepting the general reasoning as presented above, one critique suggests that societies will not reap the full fruit of progress if its generation and diffusion is entirely left to self-organization. The emphasis of this critique can be placed either on generation or on diffusion. With regard to the generation of epistemic progress, it can be argued that the most important questions for research are not necessarily those whose answers will produce the greatest social benefits. That is why epistemic practices have to be steered by an external agency for the sake of the collective good, as per the argument already mentioned above. If guided exclusively by prices and money, in turn, economic practices may fail to generate certain goods that are necessary to satisfy even basic material needs. Throughout much of the twentieth century, water and energy supply, as well as transport and communication infrastructure, have been the key examples for 'goods' for the production of which individual agency on markets is insufficient and collective agency is required.

With regard to the diffusion of progress, epistemic practices have long been guided by the commitment to sharing new knowledge. But the increasing organization of knowledge production inside business organizations has limited access to, and usability of, knowledge. Current debates about knowledge as a common good to which access should be free are based on classical assumptions about knowledge as progressing and about progress through knowledge. The diffusion of economic progress, in turn, can be found wanting when profits from production lead to increases in social inequality, when the fruit of progress is appropriated by few rather than all, and often even at the expense of many, as discussed above. Throughout much of the twentieth century, the most significant way of addressing such imbalance has been taxation of business revenue and subsequent distributive measures. In sum, this form of critique accepted the hegemonic notion of epistemic and economic progress, but saw the need for correcting mechanisms with a view to enhancing the society-wide benefit. Many such mechanisms have been widely applied, but curiously have often been abandoned over the past few decades – a question that will require further scrutiny in chapter 5.

A second, more critical argument emphasized negative consequences of the search for epistemic and economic progress as undertaken according to the dominant view. Epistemic and economic practices may even be organized for the generation of progress, as sketched above, but they do not only generate progress but also negative, regressive effects. 'Side effects', 'externalities', 'unintended consequences', and *effets pervers* have been terms proposed from different traditions of thought to name what are rather similar phenomena. Modern technology creates benefits but also hazards of various kinds, from pollution levels in industry and traffic to the risks associated with nuclear technology, most recently re-evoked by the Fukushima disaster in

Japan. Even though these negative effects were never unknown, for a long time the debate about them was dominated by two convictions: that the benefits far outweigh the risks; and that the innovative human mind that created and applied these technologies would also come up with feasible solutions to reduce the negative effects or to keep them under control. From the 1960s onwards, the ecological debate strongly and increasingly challenged those convictions.

From within this debate, but merging with other historico-philosophical approaches, a third, yet more profound, critique emerged. It suggested that the pursuit of those progress-oriented epistemic and economic practices radically transformed both human beings and the earth we live on. We encounter a strong version of this theorem in Theodor W. Adorno and Max Horkheimer's *Dialectic of Enlightenment* of 1944. The authors see the Enlightenment as embracing a philosophy of the subject, in which the individual human being first embarks on radical doubt, questioning everything that is except his own doubt, and then recreates the world for his own purpose. Even though Adorno and Horkheimer situate the full power of the transformative project at the moment when this philosophy allies itself with industry and capitalism, they identify the sources of the thus-conceived modern project in the Enlightenment. One and a half decades later, Hannah Arendt, in *The Human Condition*, locates the possibility of full elaboration of an instrumental attitude to the earth and human life at the moment when a human being can for the first time look at the world from the outside, due to space travel. From this moment onwards, the earth can be perceived as an object, from a distance, rather than as the condition for life itself. More recent, post-Kuhnian science studies see knowledge practices less in terms of a discovery of pre-existing features of nature than as interventions in nature that create and enhance specific perspectives on the 'object' at the expense of others.

In a long-term perspective, this debate reflects on the way in which epistemic-economic activity has massively transformed the world. The graphic depiction of economic growth from 1820 to the present, as provided above, would look even more impressive if one used material indicators such as: the amount of coal, gas and oil extracted from the earth; the amount of earth moved to produce building materials; the length of railway and asphalted road networks; the number of cars in use; the share of the earth's surface sealed by buildings or infrastructure; and so on. The transformation of the world – the appropriate title of Jürgen Osterhammel's recent book about the nineteenth century – has experientially been expressed early on and in a great variety of ways. The theme can be found in Goethe's *Faust* (see, for instance, Marshall Berman's 1982 reading in *All that is Solid Melts into Air*). Riding on a train and seeing trains crossing the country has altered the perception of time and space. The novelty of, and similarity between, industrial and urban movements has been praised in artistic currents such as futurism and has been visually captured in films such as *Modern Times*. It was a concern in nature-oriented movements around the turn of the nineteenth century. However, it has not been addressed as a comprehensive transformation of the earth before the 1950s – comprehensive here indicating that the earth itself is of concern, not only limited movements on its surface. Since the 1980s, though, human-made climate change and major nuclear accidents have become the key topics that changed the terms of the debate. In both cases, it is plausible to assume that the risks created are such that the inhabitability of the earth itself, or at least major regions of it, is at stake and that they are of a long-term nature, with possible moments of irreversibility. If so, then the consequences of a transformation effected by past human action move out of the reach of future human action.

In contrast to the first two critiques of the effects of epistemic-economic progress, this third critique does not lend itself easily to an assessment of benefits and losses that can balance in some way. In epistemic terms, the knowledge-intervention transforms the 'object' in such a way that it comes to conform to the knowing-subject's perspective due to the intervention. In historical terms, the transformation of the earth may signal an epochal change of such a kind that the very conditions for human agency have been altered. The assessment of progress as a normatively positive change over time requires some stability of concepts; these transformations, though, are of such a kind that they demand new concepts. Returning to the *problématiques* from which we started, paradoxes arise: the search for increasing the knowledge on which human social life can reliably be based is answered by transforming the earth in such a way that it corresponds to the kind of knowledge that is available to us humans. Rather than using reason to understand the human condition, the human condition is transformed to make it intelligible to a certain kind of reason. The search for satisfying human material needs, in turn, is answered by transforming the earth in such a way that needs satisfaction may become for ever impossible (at least in parts of the earth), without possibility of return to the earlier situation. To understand why these paradoxes could arise, we need to return to the analysis of the supposed dynamics of progress according to the strong concept.

Progress Without End

Epistemic and economic progress were to be secured through the self-organization of knowledge-seeking and needs-satisfying practices, as shown above. Epistemic practices were initially oriented towards searching for knowledge for the sake of understanding and based on communication between knowledge producers, but have increasingly been mobilized for instrumental purposes of business and state government. For economic practices, in turn, it has long been suggested that, rather than organizing explicitly for needs satisfaction, it is preferable to use the indirect tools of markets and competition to increase the wealth of nations, disconnected from any substantive aim. This detaching of economic thinking from material production and substantive concerns has been a dominant, even though not linear, trend over the past two centuries. It meant that ends moved out of sight, and endlessness emerged as a possibility. As plausible as the reasoning may have appeared in Adam Smith's and some of his contemporaries' writings at the time, it is arguably at the source of the paradoxes described above.

Without entering into what is an elaborate discussion between philosophy and psychology, one probably can assume that material needs are reasonably finite. In the context of the current financial-economic crisis in Europe, media reporting sometimes suggests that living standards have fallen back to levels comparable to those during the 1990s or even the 1980s. In other words, it is suggested that there has been material regress. Such a statement simply traces the development of some indicator, mostly the GDP that due to the crisis has fallen back to the point in time when it first reached the level of today. For most West European regions, however, a satisfactory level of living had arguably been reached for the majority of the population by that moment in the past that is referred to. The GDP as a standard measure of progress, thus, hardly reflects levels of well-being. From the 1970s onwards, accordingly, the use of the GDP as a measure of material progress has been criticized and terms such as 'qualitative growth' have been introduced. More recently, the Human Development Index has been proposed by South Asian economists as an alternative measure of needs satisfaction, including life expectancy, education and income data, and is used by the United Nations Development Programme. Debate around notions such as *buen vivir* in the Andean countries of Latin America and *décroissance* in Europe, too, point to the dissatisfaction with the reasoning that identifies potentially endless economic growth with perpetually improving the satisfaction of material needs.[2]

Despite these reflections and the elaboration of alternatives, however, economic growth remains central as a measure of material progress. A drop in the European GDP by a few percentage points in some of the years after 2008 was seen as a sign of deep crisis. A decrease of the growth of the Brazilian GDP to 2 per cent per year is taken to suggest policy failure. We need to ask, therefore, whether the persistence of this indicator points to, if not the need, then the desire for ever further material enrichment. There are two popular expressions that point to such an attitude. It used to be very widespread for – European – parents to say that they wished their children to have better lives than they themselves had. This is, maybe not exclusively but significantly, a demand for material progress. But it also used to be expressed against the background of true hardship that the parents had experienced. The expression is much less used today, and not only because European children today are less likely to have better living conditions than their parents, but also because they do not need to have them. To have roughly the same would in most cases be good enough. In the United States, in turn, the expression 'keeping up with the Joneses' employs a social comparison in space, not in

[2]The notion of *buen vivir* even implies a rejection of much of that which long was considered as progress. Further progress, in the sense of improving living conditions, would then be seen more as a return than as a move forward.

time like the generational comparison. Furthermore, it is an expression of envy with regard to strangers, rather than of care with regard to next-of-kin. It points to an increase in material consumption not to satisfy one's material needs, but to satisfy one's pride or self-regard in relation to others.

Both of these expressions point to possible driving forces for economic growth. If valid, the latter force would indeed sustain growth without end, whereas the former would cease to exist once parents had reasonable living conditions that they would like only to see sustained for future generations. But their actual impact on economic growth depends on the institutional context in which they are active. Of the two forces, the former has a substantive measure, namely a degree of needs satisfaction, whereas the latter does not – it only has a comparative measure in relation to others.

A capitalist economy has often been described as an economy without substantive measure. It is constitutively expansionist. With the emphasis on markets regulating production by drawing on the interest of the individual economic agent to produce that which finds demand, economic thought inaugurated the idea that the question of satisfaction of needs can best be answered indirectly. Rather than trying to determine through some agency what the needs are and then organizing production towards satisfying them, a mechanism, the outcome of market exchange – whether products are sold and at which price – will direct individually autonomous producers to produce that which is needed. There is no need here to discuss the numerous assumptions that need to be made to sustain the argument that markets will increase the 'wealth of nations' by the work of some 'invisible hand'. It only needs to be underlined that the exchange mechanism substitutes for any explicit substantive judgement about the satisfaction of needs.

Nevertheless, classical political economy retained a substantive anchoring through its labour theory of value.

Ultimately, the available amount of labour posed a constraint to production. One looked for new ways of maximizing 'wealth' precisely because there was scarcity and needs satisfaction was to be improved upon. With a different perspective, John Maynard Keynes, too, thought that an economy had a given potential, and economic thought should be devoted to devise ways of maximizing the use of this potential, otherwise needs remained unsatisfied. For him, the under-utilization of the economic potential due to unemployment was the key problem.

In between classical thinking and Keynesianism, Marx and marginal utility theorists had taken more radical steps of de-linking economic action from needs satisfaction. In Smith's thinking, the usefulness of products would, by and large, determine demand for them. The market mechanism was nothing but a maximizing device, based on the expression of need for useful products. Marx explicitly decoupled use-value from exchange-value, and the dynamics of the economy was now determined by the pressure on profits due to competition and class struggle. Rather than an 'invisible hand' maximizing utility, the logic of economic action turned 'behind the backs' of the actors into a search for profit for profit's sake. Obviously, Marx kept the substantive anchoring in the value of labour, but, rather than enhancing utility, this anchoring would increase contradictions and contribute to capitalism's collapse. In marginal utility theory, the anchor was finally lifted. Utility now became entirely subjective, not rooted in anything else than the preferences of the market actors. The distinction between classes being abolished, every economic actor became a preference maximizer.

The economic practices that emerge from such a conception engender the endless pursuit of pseudo-rational pseudo-mastery, as Cornelius Castoriadis once put it. Material progress had been understood as the increase of mastery, and this was problematic on its own terms. Two centuries later, the object of mastery keeps undergoing transformations in the process, and the purpose of mastery has been evicted from public debate. There is still progress of knowledge and material progress, and in its specific instantiations it often is neither difficult to identify nor even to measure. What has become difficult, if not impossible, is to see it as part of a comprehensive progress of history.

3

Progress as Struggle under Conditions of Ambivalence

The Imaginary of Social and Political Progress: Equal Freedom

Unlimited progress of knowledge and unprecedented material progress were key components of the strong concept of progress as it arose during the eighteenth century. On their own, however, they would probably not have sparked the expectation of a general liberation of humankind from the constraints of the past. The hopes for a radical break with the experiences of the past and the opening of the path for a bright future were similarly motivated by the expectation of social and political progress of a kind history had not yet seen.

In the preceding chapter, I have characterized epistemic-economic progress as marked by a particular interpretation of the Enlightenment commitment to freedom and reason, namely as geared towards mastery by means of autonomy. Social and political progress, in contrast, can be characterized as driven by the commitment to autonomy. Freedom is at the centre of the new hope and expectations. Humankind will finally exit from immaturity, to refer again to Kant. The enthusiasm was generated by the possibilities that would emerge with freedom: freedom as self-realization in personal terms and freedom as political self-determination in collective terms.

In later debate, such enabling notions of freedom were sometimes referred to as 'freedom for', namely for realizing some substantive goals in personal or collective life, and distinguished from notions of freedom as absence of constraints, 'freedom from'. Today, we see these debates as part of the political tradition of liberalism, and over time the fervour in the struggle of 'freedom for' was mitigated by a more sober emphasis on 'freedom from'. This emphasis on freedom from constraints was regarded as crucial, first, because the Old Regime, as one came to say after the French Revolution, had imposed constraints that needed to be removed, denying freedom of expression, freedom of religion or freedom of commerce. And it remained significant, second, because post-revolutionary regimes granted freedoms in an unequal way. Emancipation, therefore, was necessary to achieve equal freedom for everyone: emancipation of the slaves, of the Jews, of women, of workers. Let us thus first discuss social and political progress as 'freedom from'.

In this sense, the agenda of progressive socio-political transformation had been fully formulated by the end of the eighteenth century. But even though attempts were made, for instance, to establish free and equal suffrage for women and men and to emancipate the slaves, such as in the Haitian Revolution, this agenda was far from realized. The consolidation of regimes after the Vienna Congress of 1815 in Europe and after the accomplishment of state independence in America, South and North, witnessed both the denial of some freedoms and the unequal granting of others. We can see equal freedom as the founding commitment of the new societies that were emerging from Enlightenment and revolutions. But since equal freedom was not realized anywhere,

future social and political progress came to be identified
with the realization of equal freedom, to occur in processes
of emancipation. It came to be seen as the *telos* of the new
society, and the notion that modernity is a project that can
be completed arose in such a conceptual context.[1] Equal
freedom was at the core of the imaginary of social and political progress.

An important feature of the concept of equal freedom in
the sense of 'freedom from' is that it can supposedly be
'measured'. The standard 'measure' of both freedom and
equality is a legal one in the form of rights. Individual
freedom is a function of the rights that an individual holds.
Equality exists when all individuals in a given society and
polity – a qualification that I need to return to below – hold
the same rights. In this form, equal freedom is today
enshrined in many state constitutions, and progress can be
measured by comparing those constitutions with earlier legal
arrangements, as well as by confronting the constitutional
commitments with actual social and political practices.

In chapter 1, the need to make a distinction between
autonomy and domination in our attempt at reviewing the
history of progress was announced. In chapter 2, this distinction was employed by showing that domination was a
goal of epistemic-economic progress – as mastery over nature
– and also turned out to be a major means of achieving such
progress. With regard to social and political progress, the
relation between autonomy and domination, in a first consideration, takes a different form: liberation from domination in terms of achieving freedom and equality becomes a
relatively straightforward indicator of progress. It is the most

---

[1] In this understanding, namely with the emphasis on 'freedom
from', social and political progress is not endless in contrast to –
some versions of – epistemic and economic progress.

fundamental normative commitment upheld in contemporary societies – under conditions of modernity, if one wants to use this term. Wherever formal discrimination between categories of persons exists, such as it did in South Africa under apartheid, such arrangements are today under strong pressure from critique and in high need of justification that most often is difficult or impossible to provide.

While fundamental and necessary, however, such a formal, politico-juridical understanding of social and political progress is also insufficient. Or in other words, the emphasis on 'freedom from' does not cover the full range of expectations for social and political progress that emerged in the late eighteenth century. 'Freedom for' may not be the best term for characterizing that which is still missing when 'freedom from' has been achieved, but it points to a lack in the imaginary of social and political progress as formal equal freedom only.

Philosophical and sociological debate has long been devoted to detecting unfreedom and inequality beyond formal rules, early examples being Etienne de la Boétie's *Discourse on Voluntary Servitude* for the former, and Jean-Jacques Rousseau's *Discourse on the Origins of Inequality* for the latter. 'Conformism' and 'anomie' are terms, as elaborated by Alexis de Tocqueville and Emile Durkheim respectively, which refer to unfreedom, which is possible even under conditions of formal freedom. If we relate them to Max Weber's concern about 'life-conduct', the possibilities for which he saw as limited by the 'iron cage' of modern capitalism, we see how possibilities for self-realization can be undermined under certain social conditions. The very term 'social inequality', to which measuring devices such as the Gini index are attached today, aims to also identify inequality under conditions of formal equality. Some of these forms of unfreedom and inequality may be due to domination, a domination of a different kind than the ones from

which emancipation was achieved, and in need of being
detected by different means. To return to the South African
example: high social inequality under apartheid was largely
due to the regime of formal domination expressed in apartheid, but it persists two decades after the abolition of formal
political inequality.[2]

Thus a distinction between formal domination, understood as a hierarchical relation between one category of
persons and another, and other forms of domination is
required. The identification of such other forms of domination has been a key theme in critical sociology. A classic
example from the sociology of education is the demonstration that children from lower social classes are likely to
achieve less at school, despite formal equal access and equal
treatment. Critical sociology denounced this 'hidden'
form of domination and often claimed to reveal its alleged
social function, such as elite reproduction or a requirement
of capitalist reproduction. Such critique was – and is –
significant because it points to lacking possibilities of self-
realization. But it tended to diminish the difference between
a situation in which there is formal equality and one in
which there is formal discrimination. By implication, in its

[2] In what follows, I will repeatedly return to the example of South
Africa because the apartheid regime was an extraordinary case of
formal domination, and its rather sudden demise lets the question
of progressive social transformation after the end of formal domination stand out starkly. A contrasting case is Brazil. A republic
committed to progress since 1889, according to its flag, Brazil is
a society marked by high degrees of inequality going back to
colonial history, but over the past century it has had less entrenched
forms of formal domination compared to many other societies,
making the identification of, and struggle against, other forms of
domination a key issue.

denunciatory posture, it also tended to suggest that a systemic feature is the cause of this domination. Both of these moves are problematic: the former denigrates the significance of past progress towards equal freedom. The latter can be seen to imply that public justifications of institutional arrangements are a mere facade of little significance.

How significant justifications are can be gathered from the fact that, even when they are based on the general commitment to equal freedom, current institutions deviate from this commitment under specific circumstances that are seen to justify unequal treatment. Examples are: arguments about merit to justify unequal treatment; the present generation's appropriation of wealth acquired by an earlier generation through inheritance; the present generation's use of resources at the expense of future generations; arguments about past injustice to justify unequal treatment in the present (positive discrimination, affirmative action); the legitimation of boundaries beyond which the commitment to equal freedom does not apply, such as state boundaries. Some of these arguments can be seen as leading to domination, such as social inequality perpetuated by inheritance laws, but others are intended to combat domination, such as affirmative action rules. Once one moves beyond formal equal freedom, one can recognize a variety of different configurations of freedom and equality. In comparison with emancipation from formal domination, social and political progress is much more difficult to assess in many of these configurations, and such assessments must be made by interpreting reality in the light of the justifications provided for those configurations.

For present purposes, social and political progress will be analysed along two dimensions. First, such progress can aim at overcoming formal domination. Under conditions of formal domination, the reaching of formal equal freedom is an important goal of progress (close to the meaning of 'freedom from'). Secondly, however, formal equal freedom does not necessarily provide suitable social conditions for personal self-realization and collective self-determination (which can be understood as the social and political meanings of 'freedom for'). Formal equal freedom may be a useful precondition for self-realization and self-determination, but it is not necessarily sufficient for self-realization, as Axel Honneth convincingly argues, and it may even contribute to creating a social situation that undermines the possibilities for self-realization. This said, the reasoning will proceed in three steps. First, historical configurations of freedom and equality will be analysed to see whether they can be compared with regard to what is here called *social progress*, namely the creation of conditions amenable to personal self-realization.[3] Towards that end, sociological indicators for effective freedom and equality within and beyond the formal understanding of domination have to be developed and applied. Secondly, *political progress*, in particular, will be discussed in terms of the capacity for self-determination in setting the rules for the life in common. Here, freedom is one measure, namely as the capacity of the political *self* to determine those rules, but another one is mastery, namely as the capacity of the self to effectively *determine* those rules. As a result, thirdly, an ambivalence is identified that underlies the struggle to interpret and realize social and political progress and that critical theory, by and large, has failed to recognize and acknowledge.

[3] Axel Honneth uses the term 'moral progress' for explorations of roughly the same phenomenon. When wanting to make distinctions between dimensions of progress, however, the term 'moral progress' is too comprehensive to be applied to one dimension alone.

Social Progress: Inclusion and Individualization

The increase of freedom and equality is often seen as the most appropriate measure for social progress. The history of western societies, in turn, more precisely of North America and Western Europe, is considered to mark the progressive realization of the objective of equal freedom for all, with modern societies having institutionalized freedom. This view is not entirely wrong: increase of freedom and equality should be an indicator of social progress and it did historically happen in the West; critical theory has tended to discard this view prematurely. But it is not entirely valid either, mostly because it equated freedom and equality with rights, thus privileging a formal juridical understanding, and additionally because it 'measured' freedom and equality within formally constituted societies, ultimately defined by state institutions, disregarding inter-societal relations.

This standard view of social progress and its projection onto the history of western societies has often – and often convincingly – been criticized, but it has not been replaced by a more adequate understanding of social progress, one with the help of which historical-comparative analysis could arrive at a more nuanced view of social progress in history. The most promising attempt in this direction, as elaborated by Axel Honneth among others, is arguably the one that considers individualization and inclusion as the phenomena through which freedom and equality present themselves experientially, thus making the question amenable to socio-historical analysis. Exercising due caution with regard to these terms, this approach will be used to guide the following reflections on social progress. As we shall see, the history of western societies looks less progressive when regarded in this way, also less progressive than Honneth believes, but the struggle for progress within it remains recognizable.

In which way can the concepts of inclusion and individualization help us in assessing historical social progress? As a first step, they just appear as different terms for equality and freedom. Inclusion would then mean that human beings – individuals or groups – become members of a society with equal rights in relation to all other members. Individualization would mean that human beings can develop their life-projects on their own, without being conditioned or determined by others. Individual rights are an important condition for individualization, endowing the singular being with some degree of independence from others. In both regards, thus, some emphasis on rights is maintained. However, the new terms go beyond an exclusive focus on rights, and this is their main merit. They allow us to identify situations of lack of inclusion even when all members of a society have equal rights. In recent sociological debate, the term 'social exclusion' is used to capture such situations. And they permit the exploration of a lack of actual individualization, even when individual rights abound. Conformism and anomie, as mentioned above, but also alienation, were historical terms for capturing social situations in which self-realization was hampered despite the existence of significant individual rights.[4] In this

[4] In Axel Honneth's approach, inclusion and individualization emerge as criteria for progress after, first, he increased the significance of his central notion of recognition towards becoming a condition for human autonomy and, second, when this more comprehensive social theory was employed to address questions of justice. At this moment, normative criteria were required to assess the conditions for autonomy and the state of justice. The reference to inclusion and individualization is Honneth's answer to this requirement. It should be noted that, for Honneth, rights are a mode of recognition and as such can enhance inclusion and individualization, but on their own they are insufficient to provide that comprehensive recognition that is needed for autonomy and justice.

sense, inclusion and individualization keep equality and freedom as the central concerns, but widen the perspective on their realization. Furthermore, in contrast to equality and freedom, inclusion and individualization are processual terms. They invite us to look at the events and processes through which inclusion and individualization increase – or decrease. Thus they are apt for a historical analysis of social change and of the progress – or regress – that occurs in the course of social change.

Given these reflections, we are prepared for a look at social progress through the historical increase of inclusion and individualization. This shall be done in a sequence of steps, starting with the more familiar legal aspects. As an increase in formal equality, inclusion has been a key feature of social transformations over the past two centuries. As mentioned above, one has to keep in mind that inclusion was denied to the majority of residents in those parts of the globe where the combined effects of the scientific, industrial and political revolutions were most pronounced: Europe and the Americas. The discrepancy between a socio-political imaginary of equality and freedom and the reality of formal inequality and restricted liberties lent itself, historically, to struggles for inclusion and individualization and, conceptually, for reading social progress in these regions in this light. In more detail, by 1800, only male property-owning heads of households were full citizens of 'modern societies'. Workers found recognition as rights holders and as contributors to the collective good through struggles from the 1830s to the 1970s. Women found recognition as citizens between 1919 and the end of the Second World War; they gained equal civil rights to men often only as late as the 1960s and 1970s; and during the same period they gained rights to their body through the legalization of divorce and abortion that ended their being trapped by legal force in unwanted personal relations. After 1917, processes of inclusion in some respects were considerably accelerated in societies where a socialist revolution had occurred. In turn, native residents of Asian and African societies under European colonial domination were excluded from most of the rights available to residents of the imperial mainlands and to settlers. Even though the pre-colonial societies had their own forms of hierarchy and stratification, which makes comparison difficult, inclusion arguably decreased with colonization. This situation only changed with the success of decolonization after the Second World War, often called national liberation, in most cases from 1960 onwards. In sum, there has been significant social progress through legal inclusion where a formal approach to rights was adopted. But this progress only occurred after often long periods of struggle, and the imposition of European law on dominated societies led to new forms of legal exclusion.

Going beyond inclusion in terms of legal equality, the picture gets considerably more complex and normatively even more ambivalent. Arguably, the question of inclusion was first explicitly posed when European seafarers unexpectedly encountered the indigenous populations of America. It arose as the question about the inclusion, or not, of these unknown beings in humanity. If answered affirmatively, it entailed the granting of some status and rights, and thus limits to the exploitation of the new territories. But even when answered affirmatively, it entailed *recognition* as being of the same kind, concretely, as potential members of Christian humanity, not recognition as equal but different. Thus inclusion could be the beginning of processes of assimilation, from being equal to being the same. Related phenomena emerged with most, maybe all, later processes of recognition and emancipation, of workers and women, of slaves, of immigrants becoming 'Americanized' in the United States, of decolonized societies embarking on 'modernization and development'. Inclusion thus becomes conditional; being recognized is conditional on being recognizable. By implication, it is no longer certain whether inclusion unambiguously means progress.

Secondly, taking a closer look at the processes of inclusion across the nineteenth and the early twentieth centuries, those that provided the basis for the view of inclusion as social progress, another ambiguity emerges. The increasing recognition of all adult residents as equal members of a society in Europe and the Americas, as expressed in universal suffrage, for instance, was accompanied by drawing stronger or new boundaries with an *outside*. This outside was either other national societies, mostly in Europe, making the move from one to another society more difficult. Or, in the Americas and in other so-called settler societies, this outside was the socially non-enfranchised groups within a society, such as the indigenous population and the descendants of slaves. Arguably, the processes of inclusion and exclusion are connected: the granting of political and social citizenship made societies depend on the loyalty and well-being of its members. Thus, it became more important to determine who the legitimate members of a society were. In other words, a more explicit definition and delimitation of the citizenry was required. As a consequence, internal recognition went along with denial of recognition to those defined as 'outside', raising the issue of justification of boundaries and of global justice and injustice. Progress, if it happened, happened inside societies, or segregated parts of societies, and often because boundaries with the outside had been set and enforced.

One may refer to equality within bounded societies as political inclusion (I will return to the issue when discussing political progress). Thirdly, where this political inclusion coincided with social inclusion, a phenomenon that up to the 1960s is mostly confined to European and socialist societies, a new form of exclusion emerged from the 1980s onwards.

Sociologists have referred to this phenomenon as *social exclusion*, emphasizing the coexistence of politico-legal equality with de facto denial of access to societal achievements for some groups. The term 'social exclusion' is much less adequate for societies in which social inclusion had earlier not been achieved. In some of those societies, such as South Africa and Brazil, the advent of equal political inclusion in the 1980s and 1990s was indeed made to coincide with steps to greater social inclusion taken by 'progressive' political majorities.

Lastly, it needs to be noted that inclusion was often claimed by and for social groups, collectivities, to whom equality had been denied – slaves, women, workers – but that it was mostly achieved in the form of *individual* rights. Thus, the collectivity that struggled for social progress as inclusion was dissolved, or at least significantly weakened, due to the achievement of inclusion. As shall be demonstrated later (in chapter 5), the fact that the reaching of formal equality entailed the disappearance of strong collectivities had an enormous impact on views of possible progress.[5]

This observation leads directly to the consideration of individualization as the second indicator of social progress.

---

[5]There are two major exceptions to this pattern: the historical formation of national societies as the collectivities that exercise collective autonomy, and the recent granting of collective rights to groups within societies. The former is better understood in terms of determining the ways of living in common and will therefore be discussed below under the heading of political progress. The latter is a recent phenomenon, which can be interpreted either as based on the insight that self-realization depends on collective forms of life, as multiculturalism, or as recognizing collective self-determination for collectivities within existing 'pluri-national' states. The former could be seen as social progress, the latter as political progress, but neither of them is without ambiguities.

The increase of individual autonomy has been a key commitment of European modernity from at least the sixteenth century onwards, even though it spread only gradually through society. From the early nineteenth century onwards, juridical change, such as the formalization of individual rights following the Declaration of the Rights of Man and of the Citizen and the granting of commercial freedom, gave a push to the orientation towards individual autonomy. Very soon, though, negative consequences in terms of the disembedding of human beings from their social contexts came to be perceived. This is the historical context in which Tocqueville would diagnose the rise of conformism as a consequence of equal freedom in US democracy; in which Marx would identify a particular form of alienation as the result of commodification, namely human relations turning into relations between things when human beings encounter each other on markets; and, somewhat later, the context in which Weber expresses his concern about the limited range of ways of conducting one's life when exposed to the rationalizing demands of modern capitalism. According to these analyses, equal individual freedom had not increased, but rather decreased individual autonomy under the socio-political conditions of the nineteenth century. One may have doubts about the adequacy of these diagnoses: possibly these observers mistakenly applied an aristocratic-bourgeois view of self-realization to the peasant and worker majority population to whom gaining equal freedom meant something different, at least as a first historical experience. Nevertheless, these analyses rightly question the immediacy of the connection between individual rights and individualization.

Subsequently, throughout the first two-thirds of the twentieth century, one can indeed observe a process of collectivization with the building of mass organizations such as parties and trade unions, often emerging from social movements of protest, and the standardizing of life expectations and forms of behaviour, enhanced through schools, mass media and mass consumption. These collective conventions and institutions of 'organized modernity' include their members as individuals, true, but they do so by means of standardizing roles and homogenizing outlooks on the world. Thus the term individualization is hardly useful to characterize the period between the 1890s and the 1950s in many societies. In turn, the social transformation that started during the 1960s is often seen as having led to highly increased individualization and new forms of individualism. Whether this new individualization can be regarded as social progress is under debate, one with which we will engage in chapter 5.

Political Progress: Individual Rights and Collective Self-Determination

Today, political progress is often considered to be indicated by individual rights and by democracy, as demonstrated by the widespread use of the slogan 'human rights and democracy', either to describe 'advanced' societies or as a claim on societies that still need to make political progress. This conception of political progress, furthermore, is seen to have been inaugurated at the end of the eighteenth century, with the above-mentioned 1789 Declaration of the Rights of Man and of the Citizen as a key event. A recent version of mapping such progress as evolutionary, even though not steady, can be found in the political-science theorem about successive waves of democratization.

But is this current understanding of political progress adequate? As suggested above, political progress should mean that better answers are given to the question of how to live together. A good answer to this question – one that is normatively acceptable and the reaching of which marks progress – has to fulfil not one but two requirements: first, the rules for living together have to be determined freely, by oneself, as the expression of the collective will of those living together. And, second, the application of those rules should result in a way of living together that is actually desired and intended. The first requirement points to autonomy, and in particular to the relation between individual and collective autonomy. The second is a question of mastery, of collectively mastering one's fate. Rather than looking at historical political progress as the increase in individual rights and democracy, therefore, the ways in which these two requirements were supposed to be fulfilled need to be explored.

Individual rights – first – were discussed above under the heading of social progress as expressions of equal freedom. In the current context, they are of concern only in so far as they relate to addressing the political *problématique*. As such, they have been seen as ambiguous. On the one hand, rights such as freedom of expression are essential for the communications that form public opinion and underlie collective decision making. Being free, furthermore, enhances the civic commitment needed to sustain the polity that provides these freedoms, a reasoning first voiced by Pericles in ancient democratic Athens. On the other hand, individual liberty can endanger the polity. If everyone only follows their own will, political deliberation may remain inconclusive and no rules for living together can be agreed upon. According to the latter reasoning, increase in liberty alone cannot unequivocally be seen as an indicator of political progress because it leaves the question of setting the rules for the life in common without an answer, as liberals from Benjamin Constant in 1819 to Isaiah Berlin in 1958 well knew.

Collective autonomy – second – requires, in turn, first of all the constitution of the collectivity that exercises collective self-determination. Historically, the textbook case of this process is the transformation of the absolute sovereignty of the monarch into the sovereignty of the people, and the key example is the French Revolution. In many situations, however, it was suggested that the boundaries of monarchical sovereignty did not coincide with the boundaries of reasonable collective self-determination. The considerations that were historically made in Europe in this regard drew on concerns about individual autonomy: if it can be difficult to reach agreement between free and unbound individuals, then a democratic polity should possibly be constituted by human beings who already have something in common, and this commonality was found in language and culture. The constitution of such cultural-linguistic communities as political subjects, therefore, was widely considered as a key component of political progress.

The subject of collective self-determination could be referred to as the people or the nation, the former term emphasizing the seizing of popular sovereignty as the form of reaching collective autonomy, the latter hinting at the existence of collectivities that lived under domination – the emancipatory struggle then being for national liberation from imperial or colonial domination. The nation-states that formed as the outcome of such struggles were seen to mark political progress due to the achievement of collective autonomy. And they were also seen as entities of equal standing towards each other, thus realizing equal freedom among collectivities in the 'international' system of states in analogy to the equal freedom of individuals within states. That their boundaries also limited the reach of equal freedom, as discussed above, was seen to be of no concern because those boundaries derived their justification from a political reasoning that had primacy over social progress, even provided the means for reaching limited social progress, indeed a bounded one.

The actual historical practice of collective self-determination – third – was radically limited by concerns for mastery. Even though the late-eighteenth-century political imaginary centrally included popular sovereignty based on free and equal universal suffrage, the idea of democracy was defeated in practice. Europe saw a restoration of the Old Regime after 1815, the newly independent republics of South America were governed by the settler elites, and the United States and Brazil furthermore maintained slavery until long into the nineteenth century, thus excluding a sizeable part of the population from political participation. Given this situation, the struggle for political progress understandably focused on reaching full and equal participation, achieved in many countries by the end of the First World War, often lost again, and regained after the end of the Second World War. Numerous countries faced persistent authoritarian or oligarchic rule to the 1980s or witnessed *coup d'états* that introduced military dictatorships during the 1960s and 1970s, most of them replaced by electoral democracies by the 1980s and 1990s.

Rather than turning this sequence of events into a narrative of an unstoppable, even though intermittent, process of democratization, it is more fruitful to ask why democracy was not introduced when its political imaginary forcefully emerged at the end of the eighteenth century. One answer to this question is the effective resistance of elites who feared to lose not only decision-making power but also many of the privileges they held before the revolutionary period. These elites were able to muster sufficient power to contain the drive towards democracy, so the argument goes. In other words, these elites attempted, temporarily successfully, to block the path of progress, which otherwise was well marked out. While being partly valid, this reasoning overlooks that justifications in terms of addressing the political *problématique* were also provided that conceived political progress in terms other than the increase of democracy.

Thus we move to discuss the history of dealing with the second requirement of political progress, namely to elaborate and implement collective rules that lead to a way of living together that is desired and intended. Stating this requirement means opening up the possibility that egalitarian-inclusive democracy is not the best means to elaborate and implement such rules. Reasoning in some such terms preceded the advent of democracy and has accompanied it all the way to the present.

Already during the eighteenth century, that is, before the epistemic-economic 'take-off' described in the preceding chapter, one accomplishment of Enlightenment reason was seen in the rationalization of state administration. When the 'advance' of Europe was considered from the outside during this period, from the angle of the Ottoman or Russian elites, for example, it was the systematic improvement of state capacity in countries such as Prussia or France that formed the centre of attention. When these reform processes merged with the claims for popular sovereignty at the end of the eighteenth century, many otherwise fairly radical Enlightenment thinkers did not advocate egalitarian-inclusive democracy. Denying any inconsistency in their reasoning, they held that the majority of the population was not sufficiently educated to make proper use of their capacity for reason. Full political participation had to wait until everyone had exited from immaturity. In many cases, one should not consider this stand as a part of elite resistance, but as a conscious justification for domination that was seen as reasonable in the given context. This justification continued to be hegemonic for colonial rule and even for relations between former colonies and former colonizers until the 1980s.

By mid-nineteenth century, the discrepancy between the political imaginary and the existing institutions had become so pronounced that the calls for democracy became more forceful. But even among the advocates, the doubts had not entirely disappeared. One can suggest that Marx was talking about a form of democracy when he invoked the dictatorship of the proletariat, but the compelling argument was not that the proletariat formed the majority of the population, but that it was the class embodying the universal interest. Such a mode of reasoning haunted the socialist tradition for a long time. Between the two world wars of the twentieth century, defenders of actual practices of collective self-determination were rare. Many intellectuals assumed that the collectivity first needed to be identified and delimited, as the working class or the nation, and the collective rules needed to be derived from the pre-defined interests of these collectivities.

It is only after the Second World War that the practices of collective self-determination were more widely accepted, not least because of the disastrous consequences of the collective essentialisms of nation and class. But even for this period, qualifications need to be added. On the one hand, the justification for limitations of democracy did not disappear entirely. It is suggested, for instance, that 'successful societies' that made considerable economic progress, such as South Korea and Brazil, laid the foundations for such progress during periods of authoritarian rule, and that political progress in terms of democracy can only be sustained once a certain degree of economic well-being has been achieved. On the other hand, the practice of collective self-determination itself had changed between the first half of the twentieth century and the second. The early century had witnessed periods of high mobilization, and now it was argued that totalitarianism was one of the outcomes of such mobilization. During the second half of the century, therefore, democracy was reinterpreted as low-level participation – 'conventional participation', as political scientists should call it – limited to elections, and political change as confined to the turnover of political personnel through those elections. All other participation was discouraged, and political apathy hailed as a precondition for democracy to be viable.

This situation was to change during the 1960s: with the success of the struggles for decolonization in Africa; with the Cuban Revolution and the radicalization of political debate in Latin America during the 1960s and 1970s; with the civil rights movement in the United States, and with the student and workers' revolts in many parts of the globe at the end of the 1960s – all signs that 'unconventional participation' had emerged and that the question of egalitarian-inclusive democracy with high intensity of participation was forcefully placed on the global political agenda. These occurrences, in turn, generated worries among the elites about the 'governability' of democracies. It became clear that political progress had been conceptualized in highly contradictory ways: as the widening and intensification of participation, on the one hand, and as the enhancement of mastery by a centralized collective agency, the state, on the other. Even though both objectives were abstractly shared by many practitioners and observers, they appeared ever more irreconcilable as they were pursued in parallel.

The Ambivalence of Social and Political Progress and the Place of Critical Theory

The preceding conceptual reflections have shown that social and political progress has its core concerns in freedom. Social and political progress, most broadly understood, is the increase in the human capacity to live life as one wants to live it, personally and collectively. The preceding historical observations, in turn, have shown that some such progress has occurred over the past two centuries. They have also shown, however, that this historical record is much more ambivalent than standard views are willing to recognize and that it poses questions for the future pursuit of social and political progress. In the final step of this chapter, an attempt will be made to identify those questions by reviewing the above findings.

The concepts of inclusion and individualization have served as useful tools for disentangling aspects of social progress, but the historico-sociological observations showed that they cannot straightforwardly serve as criteria for measuring progress for two reasons. First, the normative connotations of the key concepts are ambiguous: individualization can be seen as liberation from imposed social bonds, but it can also be related to loss of meaning. Inclusion seems to prepare the way for a social, not merely formal-legal, understanding of equality, but for this very reason it moves into proximity with terms such as 'integration' and 'assimilation', if one neglects questions about the conditions for, and modes of, inclusion. Secondly, the potentially problematic nature of the relation between the two terms is underestimated. Inclusion refers to becoming an (equal) member of a collectivity, thus standing in tension with the notion of individualization. Individualization, in turn, makes human beings differentiate themselves from others, and such differentiation can – even though it does not have to – entail hierarchization and domination.

For these reasons, it is not plausible to assume linear processes of either inclusion or individualization. Historically, processes of inclusion often went along with the erection of boundaries, and thus exclusion of others outside and often also limitations to freedom inside. In turn, individualization processes often entailed increasing social and/or cultural inequality and thus forms of exclusion. Along one line of reasoning, already discussed with regard to epistemic and economic progress, such setbacks can be analysed as unintended consequences of achieving some kind of progress. With regard to social and political matters, furthermore, progress generates regress also for other reasons, two of which are central to our concerns.

First, social and political progress is often the result of struggle. Those who benefit from existing situations of domination will be inclined to resist calls for greater egalitarian-inclusive self-determination. While the outcome of struggle may mark progress, it is also likely to entail a shift in the terrain on which struggle is led. Or in other words, a partial victory in a struggle leads to a displacement of issues rather than an all-out accomplishment. To give one example that shows two kinds of displacement: in the course of the twentieth century, the West European workers' movement achieved higher wages, better working conditions and greater social security in the course of its struggle, mobilizing the 'social critique', in the term used by Luc Boltanski and Eve Chiapello. However, these accomplishments contributed to generating routinization of work, homogenization of life-situations and other features of 'mass society', leading to alienation, which in turn mobilized the 'artistic critique' in the later twentieth century. In parallel, these accomplishments were also conditioned by separating the core industrial working class from other workers and from peasants, either through state boundaries or through partial corporatist inclusion. For both aspects, the 'regressive' transformation in the broader social setting can be seen as a response to the success of 'progressive' claims, with a view to keeping capitalist production profitable while granting social progress.

Secondly, furthermore, the pursuit of progress can also be marked by unavoidable ambivalence. This ambivalence can best be exemplified by the necessary double orientation of political progress towards freedom and mastery. There is no need to accept the argument, which is outright conservative or reactionary, that a large collectivity of human beings with naturally diverse interests and inclinations is unable to govern itself. But one does need to recognize that the idea of collective self-determination contains within itself the tension between the continuous free expression of the will of all, on the one side, and, on the other, the formation of a general will, to use Rousseau's words, and the transformation of the latter into effectively behaviour-orienting rules and institutions.

These two observations suggest that the temporality of social and political progress cannot be linear for reasons inherent in the notion of such progress itself. They also suggest that complete social and political progress cannot be attained; it is not a project bound to be completed. Achieved progress on some aspect is likely to generate regress on some other because of the lack of adequate knowledge of its consequences, because of the displacement of struggle and/or because of the shift in emphasis when reinterpreting an unavoidable ambivalence. In subsequent chapters, the consequences of this insight for the reinterpretation of progress today will be explored. Before doing so, it is worth emphasizing that critical theory of contemporary society has often been less than convincing, precisely because it failed to make or accept this insight.

What do I mean by critical theory? As it emerged during the nineteenth century, social theory in general focused on the question of freedom, on the possible or likely social consequences of the institutionalization of individual freedom, from Hegel, Marx and Tocqueville onwards. By the late nineteenth century, a tension between affirmative and critical approaches to the issue had emerged. The former recognized the ambivalence but saw possibilities of reaching normatively viable ways of dealing with it; Emile Durkheim's social and political thought is a key example. The latter assumed that, under prevailing forms of socio-political organization, the idea of freedom would be undermined in practice, that a self-cancellation of the emancipatory promises of the revolutionary period would be the outcome.

In those terms, social theory in general is an exploration of social progress, as defined here. And critical theory, in particular, is that version of social theory that emphasized and denounced actual social regress, despite the promise of social progress. The critical debate about social progress was critical of the very foundations of contemporary society, from Marx's critique of political economy to the Critical Theory of the Frankfurt School to the neo-Marxism of the 1970s. It was indeed not explicitly led in terms of a debate about social progress, but the theme was embedded in a comprehensive social theory. When disentangling the dimensions of progress, as done here, a particular angle on critical theory emerges, making its shortcomings more clearly visible. I should underline, though, that the objective is not to abandon the attempt at comprehensive theory but reconstruct such theory after re-composing the components of the picture.

Implicitly, the critical debate on social progress worked with strong lines of demarcation from other dimensions of progress. It became topical in the nineteenth century against the background of the experience with economic progress. It took principled stances on the epistemic and the economic question, basically endorsing the standard view on possible steady progress of knowledge and material progress, not realized and not realizable, though, under conditions of modern society. This discrepancy between possibility and reality leads to the critique of ideology, and to the critique of political economy in particular. Social progress and its lack were explored against the background of an epistemic-economic constellation that was taken for granted. In other words, the ways in which the questions about valid knowledge and needs satisfaction should in principle be addressed did not require a specific answer from critical theory.[6] One

---

[6] The exception was Adorno who subjected knowledge production and its material offshoot, culture industry, to a totalizing critique, as seen above.

could legitimately focus on the problems with social progress that the institutional conditions created under which these answers were implemented. In the preceding chapter, I have tried to show that this stand is inadequate.

Political progress was of little direct concern in critical theory either, but for a different reason. It was assumed that adequate answers to the question about ways of living together could not be found under prevailing conditions; thus, one did not even need to search for them. A particularly striking example is Theodor Adorno criticizing Karl Mannheim in the 1930s for failing to see that formal democracy is an irrelevant surface phenomenon, only the facade of capitalist society. The widespread disdain for political philosophy in critical theory can also be understood against this background. The only relevant political issue in the present was the struggle for overcoming domination. After liberation from domination, then, in the implicit and sometimes explicit view, political questions would be unproblematically answered in free deliberation among free human beings.

In other words, the tradition of critical social theory has considered what is here defined as social matters as the centre of societal analysis and has relegated all other matters to a secondary rank: epistemic and economic matters because they were basically solved already; and political matters because they could only be solved in the future, but then unproblematically so. To disentangle the question of progress and to discuss its four dimensions separately is also an attempt to overcome the narrow pursuit of past critique and open the possibility for the identification of the key critical issues of our time.

4

The Idea of Progress
Revisited

The brief review of historical progress between 1789 and
1989 in the preceding two chapters provides a complex
picture. There has been progress but in highly varied ways.
There has been regress, too, and some consequences of past
progress appear to undermine not only the possibility for
future progress, but even the sustainability of the present
state of humankind. All this suggests that the strong concept
of progress is unlikely to be rescued. Many of the experiences over the past two centuries speak against it; and these
experiences have such an accumulated weight that we can
no longer separate our expectations radically from them. But
if we probably have to abandon the strong concept of
progress, does that mean that we need to discard any concept
of progress at all? In the light of the historical reconstruction, I shall now take a second look at the assumptions
underlying the strong concept of progress, at their core the
progressive articulation of freedom and reason. How were
these assumptions argued for, and is there anything in them
that we can maintain?

The Enlightenment Connection: Autonomy and Progress

When, in chapter 1, a brief portrait of the Enlightenment assumptions underlying the strong concept of progress was provided, I called it a caricature. Now is the moment to make the picture more nuanced with a view to identifying the ideas of historicity and historical change that might help in the reconstruction of a notion of progress for today. Along the way, the first steps of which lead from Immanuel Kant to Karl Marx, we will indeed also witness the historical transformation of the concept of progress in the light of experiences with what was seen as its application. This endeavour will also serve to better understand the ambivalence of progress pointed out in chapter 3.

In 1784, Immanuel Kant wrote two short texts which show both his commitment to the principle of autonomy and the expectation that human freedom will lead humankind on the road to progress in history. In *An Answer to the Question: 'What is Enlightenment?'* he defines the latter as the 'exit from self-incurred immaturity'. 'Idea for a Universal History from a Cosmopolitan Point of View' starts with the suggestion that we can develop a reading of history that:

> permits us to hope that if we attend to the play of freedom of the human will in the large, we may be able to discern a regular movement in it, and that what seems complex and chaotic in the single individual may be seen from the standpoint of the human race as a whole to be a steady and progressive though slow evolution of its original endowment.

This latter text will be at the centre of the following reflections.

Freedom, thus, indeed leads to progress in Kant's view, as the caricature description maintained. However, this is no short and easy road. Freedom, first of all, does not create harmony; Kant rather emphasizes the ambivalent, even contradictory, inclinations of human beings, for which he coins the term 'unsocial sociability'. Humans both want to be together with other human beings as well as to isolate themselves from others. As a consequence of the antagonism between human beings, history is marked by war, strife, greed, vanity, chaos and unruliness. But how then is progress possible? Kant has an answer to this question – maybe even two – over which his interpreters struggle.

Reading the opening sentence again, one recognizes that steady and progressive evolution is not recognizable in individual human actions, but only 'in the large'. On a closer look, Kant holds, all the discord can be shown to lead to something new. The 'resistance', namely, that human beings encounter through other human beings 'awakes all forces' in them, 'makes them overcome their laziness and [. . .] gain a rank among [their] fellow human beings'. As a result of this activity, 'the first true steps from rawness to culture' are taken; 'all talents are gradually developed; the sense of taste is formed'; and continued enlightenment can then even mark the beginning of the foundation of society as a moral whole. Thus Kant describes the mechanism, as current analytical sociology would call it, which turns individual human actions into positive collective outcomes beyond the intention of the actors.

But the explanation of the mechanism divides Kant's interpreters. On the face of it, Kant stipulates a plan of nature on the basis of the following reasoning: everything in nature has a purpose. Human beings, although having the particularity of being endowed with reason, are part of nature. Therefore, human history must have a purpose. And this purpose, to be reached in the long run, is the foundation of society as a moral whole. This is an a priori assumption that we have difficulty sharing today. And without it, Kant's notion of progress falls.

But there is another way of reading the text. In this view, Kant does not claim at all that history is actually on a steady and progressive road. In the face of the apparent complexity and chaos, rather, he explores the conditions of possibility for identifying such a road, if any. As Dipesh Chakrabarty (2000) said about Marx in *Provincializing Europe*, Kant 'does not so much provide us with a teleology of history as with a perspectival point from which to read the archives'. The reason why one should do so is existential – so as not to despair – but also practical. Kant believes that a review of positive experiences in human history can enlighten collective action, or, rather, the action of rulers in the present and thus enhance the prospect for a better future. If there is a direction in human history, therefore, it is not in any plan of nature, as we would normally understand this term,[1] but it can be gathered by current 'philosophical attempts' to review human history, using the faculty of understanding we are endowed with, with the objective of finding an answer to the question of living well together and accepting the other's autonomy.

In this reading, the 'plan of nature' is nothing that is effective without human beings contributing to it, no external device that drives human history, the latter understood as the sum of all human actions. It is something that can be detected by a 'philosophical attempt' in history, understood as 'concerned with narrating the appearances' of human

---

[1] This may be due to the fact that we are used to operating with a strong distinction between 'nature' and 'society', which Kant clearly did not. For seeing this distinction as constitutive of modernity, see Bruno Latour's *We Have Never Been Modern*.

actions. In other words, there is a relation between autonomy and reason in Kant that is foundational for progress, but it is not at all an automatic one. Human freedom left on its own has ambivalent outcomes. Reason is needed to decipher those outcomes with a view to elevating the progressive moments in human history to higher significance and make them direct future action.

Let it be noted here, for future reference, that this is politico-philosophical reason, a particular form of reason. It is within the human world, not external to it. But it is not part of the everyday 'unsocial sociability'. To maintain his hope for progress, Kant had to step out of the chaos and complexity of general human activity and prioritize a very particular human activity as a guide to reading the ways of the world.[2]

Kant's social ontology remained limited to the theorem of unsocial sociability. To resolve the problems arising from such ambiguous human inclinations, he stepped out of the social realm and resorted to political institutions, and he reasoned about them in terms of conditions of possibility. Furthermore, he had no view of any temporal dynamics in the play of those human inclinations. They appear as an anthropological constant. The temporal dynamics that one finds in his writings – the reason why one can refer to them as a progressive philosophy of history – is entirely related to the detection of progress on the way to a moral order of society, as revealed through a perspectival reading of history.

---

[2] In a more detailed reading, this observation would be related to Kant's distinction between *Vernunft* (reason) and *Verstand* (normally translated as understanding). The distinction is not taken up here; I refer to both capacities as 'reason', providing a broad and admittedly sweeping view of Enlightenment thought (see the note in chapter 1).

Half a century after Kant's death, the combined effect of the political and economic transformations since the late eighteenth century had created a socio-political situation that appeared to confirm Kant's (and in general the Enlightenment's) assumption that socio-political arrangements are constituted by human beings through their actions. But experiences with such arrangements had suggested that new social phenomena were emerging as outcomes of human action. One now needed to see whether these outcomes spelt progress or not.

Maintaining the basic assumptions of late eighteenth century thought, scholars became increasingly convinced that one could now see and know more about the socio-political transformations by the mid-nineteenth century. Alexis de Tocqueville (1835/40) analysed the social impact of democracy, and he advanced a notion of the direction of history when he suggested that (what one now calls) democratization would not come to a halt before equal universal suffrage was reached. For him, this was inescapable; whether it was progress is less certain. Lorenz von Stein (1850) observed the emergence of 'social movements' in response to the economic changes related to the liberty of commerce and the rise of a market economy. In both cases, the creation of specific institutional conditions for human freedom – the political vote and the economic right to buy and sell – were seen as having unleashed an unintended and unforeseen social dynamics that would need to be taken into account when considering the conditions for progress or, to speak in Kant's terms, for establishing a moral order.

The scholar who developed such a mode of thinking most forcefully at this moment was Karl Marx. For Marx, the unintentionally produced structures were the capitalist mode of production with new antagonistic classes. Rather than equally free economic actors, the new socio-political order produced a radical divide between those who owned the

means of production and those who did not. The dynamics
was unleashed by market competition, as indeed foreseen
and intended by classical political economy, and by class
struggle, which was at the centre of Marx's political concerns. Having witnessed economic crises and the deterioration of the conditions of the working classes, Marx thought
he was recognizing clear trends in historical change as a
consequence of this dynamics, but no longer linear progress.
Well acquainted with Hegel's thought, however, he was also
able to consider end-points of certain trends, the reaching of
which would lead to a change of direction. Combining
economic analysis and philosophy of history with political
analysis, he elaborated his particular view of historical
directedness that foresaw movement towards the point of
unsustainability of the capitalist mode of production, for
reasons of both competition and class struggle, and subsequently the emergence of a new historical horizon, entirely
open and determined by free human beings in free
association.

In other words, the Kantian problem is well recognizable
in Marx's writings. Like Kant, Marx was committed to
human agency, and similarly he recognized the 'antagonism'
in human social relations. For him, though, the negative
consequences of this antagonism could not be overcome by
an institutional design pulled from a selective reading of
historical experiences. The structures and dynamics that he
identified were too powerful for such a hope. But, following
Kant's 'methodology', he searched through such dynamics
to identify the prospect for positive change. For the relation
between agency and phenomena 'in the large', this now
required situating agency within the course of the dynamics
that had been unleashed.

The tension between human agency, on the one hand, and
the identification of determining structures and dynamics,
on the other, is an unresolved dilemma in Marx's writings.

Towards the end of the nineteenth century, it led to the peculiar political phenomenon of 'revolutionary attentism' in the workers' movement, in German social democracy in particular, namely the combination of a revolutionary, that is, highly agential, self-understanding with the perceived need to wait passively until history brings forth the revolutionary moment. What I want to underline for present purposes is that this tension is never entirely absent in Marx: in what sense progress is the inevitable direction of history, and in what sense it will need to be brought about by human action, of which we can never be sure whether it will happen or not, remains undetermined.

In the sober analysis of *Capital*, to take one example, which as a 'critique of political economy' aims to uncover the contradictions of a capitalist mode of production, the 'tendency of the rate of profit to fall' has often been taken as the core argument for demonstrating the inescapably self-destructive tendencies of capitalism. However, Marx adds to this analysis the enumeration of 'countervailing factors', many of which can contingently arise at any moment and lead to a transformation of capitalism – possibly both unintended and unforeseen – rather than its end.

In political pamphlets, the expression of the tension between a compelling driving force of history and the intervention of human agency can take dramatic shape. It is widely accepted that the *Communist Manifesto* of 1848, co-authored with Friedrich Engels, is a statement of historical progress in which class struggle drives history towards communism. The fact that both the bourgeoisie, historically, and the proletariat, in the future, are hailed for their heroic actions does not change this interpretation because the activities of both classes are effective and successful in so far as they are in harmony with the progressive course of history. This common reading, however, overlooks the doubts that Marx and Engels, too, had about the history of humanity.

At the very beginning of the pamphlet, but nevertheless mostly overlooked, we find the conjecture that class struggle may also end – indeed, sometimes has ended – with the 'common ruin of the contending classes'. This theme of defeat and disaster, though marginal, has never disappeared from the Marxian tradition. In 1915, Rosa Luxemburg analysed the world-historical situation after the beginning of the First World War and the vote of social-democratic members of the German *Reichstag* in favour of war loans, in terms of a stark alternative: 'either transition to socialism or regression into barbarism' (Luxemburg 2000 [1916]). Ultimately, Marx and those who followed him do not claim to know the course of history because human beings can always act otherwise – for better, or for worse.

Critiques: Autonomy Undermining Progress

These observations on Marxian thinking lead us to considerations about doubts on progress that have coexisted with the concept of progress since its invention, but were to accumulate in Europe in the later nineteenth century and, in particular, in the years after the First World War. The critique of progress on which such doubts were based could take very different forms. One can criticize the general idea that the conditions for human life on earth can be lastingly improved, or one can criticize the more specific idea that human autonomy leads to progress. Furthermore, one can draw different conclusions from those critiques: in the former case, one might turn away from any attempt at improvement, or one can aim for as much betterment as one can reach in one's own time. In the latter case, one can reject the very idea of organizing human social life on the basis of autonomy, or one can consider additional conditions under which human interaction on the basis of autonomy becomes collectively beneficial.

The view that no attempt at improvement should even be attempted has been brilliantly reconstructed by Albert Hirschman as the rhetoric of reaction. The term 'reactionary', namely, entered our political language precisely as a denomination for those who reacted against the commitment to progress that emerged forcefully from the late eighteenth century onwards. This rhetoric, Hirschman demonstrates, mobilizes three figures of speech: attempts at betterment are futile because the human condition cannot be altered; they are perverse because they lead to unintended consequences that entail a deterioration of the human condition; and/or they are dangerous because they might undermine normative accomplishments that already exist.

The more specific view that human autonomy paves the way for progress has similarly been criticized from the moment that Enlightenment thinkers had spread that idea. Commenting on the French Revolution from across the Channel, Edmund Burke (1993 [1790]) would say a few years after Kant: 'The effect of liberty to individuals is that they may *do* what they *please*; we ought to see what it will *please them to do*, before we risk congratulations.' Some of Burke's French contemporaries, such as Bonald and Maistre, held stronger views: they would not even want to see what it might please individuals to do because a well-ordered society is an organic whole that assigns individuals their places and possibilities for action. Compared with such rejection of autonomy, Burke moderately raises a valid concern: if human beings truly exercise their free will, there is little we can know beforehand about the outcome of this exercise. We may indeed say that both Kant and Marx recognized the issue and invoked politico-philosophical reason or pointed to competition and class struggle as ways to direct or understand, respectively, the consequences of autonomy.

In the first chapter, we saw that the strong notion of progress suggests that lasting improvement is both *possible and probable*, and that it *will* be achieved through human autonomy. For the purposes of reconstruction, I provisionally suggest that we need to maintain, in general, that betterment is *possible in principle* and, specifically, that it *needs* to be achieved under conditions of autonomy, even though additional considerations on the workings of autonomy can be introduced. We may call this the minimum condition for a weak notion of progress. If we abandoned any notion of possible improvement, we would have no concept of progress at all any longer. If we abandoned the commitment to autonomy, we would jettison the core normative principle of modernity.

In this light, we may consider those views that hold that improvement is not possible and/or that it cannot be achieved under conditions of autonomy as *external critiques* of progress. In turn, we may consider those views that hold that the direction of history is not necessarily marked by progress and that regress, too, is possible and/or that progress does not emerge automatically under conditions of autonomy as *internal critiques* of progress. For our purposes, the internal critiques are much more relevant than the external ones because they invite for rethinking, whereas the external ones suggest abandoning the concept of progress.

The internal critiques are therefore at the centre of our reconstruction, but a note of caution needs to be added. Sometimes it is not easy to identify whether a critique is internal or external. Does Burke, for instance, raise his question rhetorically to suggest that we should not even think about building societies and polities on individual autonomy? Or does he invite an investigation of the socio-political consequences of doing so? The former would be an external critique, the latter an internal one. In some cases, as we shall see, thinkers start out from a commitment to autonomy but conclude that it cannot be maintained. For reasons of openness of the investigation, we, too, shall not a priori rule out that latter possibility.

As the brief confrontation of Marx with Kant has shown, the conceptualization of progress changes with historical context. One could think that this is due to a simple fact: as time passes, there are more historical events to consider in the assessment of whether there has been progress or not, thus the judgement is likely to change. But there is also a more specific contextual change: the Enlightenment authors saw themselves as writing at the dawn of the era of autonomy. To exaggerate slightly, they had only expectations, not experience. Marx, in turn, is writing in the light of experiences with autonomy that he wishes to analyse. He sees how autonomy via commodification turns into alienation, to put it crudely. In other words, expectations were set free from the constraints of experience at around 1800, and the horizon was wide open. By mid-century, experiences had partly caught up with expectations. One could return to defining expectations in the light of experience, even though the horizon remained somewhat open.

It is fruitful to continue this contextual analysis by briefly looking at Max Weber's reflections in the early twentieth century. Weber is the most important analyst of the rise of occidental rationalism, a thesis on long-term social change with a strong direction. As he famously formulated in one of his key research questions: 'what concatenation of circumstances has led to the fact that in the Occident, and here only, cultural phenomena have appeared which – as at least we like to imagine – lie in a direction of development of universal significance and validity?' There is indeed both a temporal and a spatial direction here. Phenomena appear in one place and develop there, but then they spread to presumably gain universal significance.

At the same time in terms of his philosophy of social science and methodology, Weber is the one among the 'classical' sociologists who was least inclined to postulate laws of social change or the existence of large-scale social phenomena that determine human action. Human beings and the ways in which they give meaning to their lives and their relations with others were the centre of his attention. His ambition was to reach an understanding of large-scale, long-term durable social phenomena ('in the large', as Kant had put it) starting out from the meaningful action of human beings. *The Protestant Ethic*, with all its flaws, remains a highly instructive document for – or maybe a monument to – such an attempt.

For the purpose of the reasoning here, the key observation on this text is this: Weber starts out from the way human beings give meaning to their lives and then demonstrates how the actions they pursue in relation to their world-interpretation transform the world in such a way that further work at giving meaning is neither necessary nor effective in any way. This is the long-term historical connection through which a world-interpretation, the Protestant ethic, brought about a rigid set of institutions, modern capitalism: 'the spirit has escaped from the cage'. Subsequently, Weber talks about the mechanical foundations of victorious capitalism and uses temporal expressions such as 'no longer' and 'finally'. This has supported the interpretation of Weber's view on rationalization as uni-directional as well as progressive, the latter because of the increase in functional efficiency, as later taken up by Talcott Parsons and the sociology of 'modernization and development', but also – with more nuance – by Jürgen Habermas in *Theory of Communicative Action*.

But Weber's views have also given rise to different interpretations. The comparative sociology of religions has inspired the recent research programme on 'multiple modernities', as pioneered by Shmuel Eisenstadt, suggesting a plurality of historical trajectories without convergence. And the underlying scepticisim about the inhabitability of a spiritless cage is in the background of strong critiques of progress, such as most significantly Adorno and Horkheimer's *Dialectic of Enlightenment*. This rather large variety of interpretations has been invited by Weber himself, who inserted an important parenthesis in his diagnosis of the present: 'whether finally, who knows?' And subsequently he added an explicit rejection of linear views of progress – or maybe of any view of progress altogether: 'No one knows who will live in this cage in the future, or whether at the end of this tremendous development, entirely new prophets will arise, or there will be a great rebirth of old ideas and ideals, or, if neither, mechanized petrification, embellished with a sort of convulsive self-importance.' If the range of possibilities is such, and if 'no one knows', the future could hardly be more undetermined.

In the light of Koselleck's felicitous metaphors, a strong irony – or should we call it a paradox? – is present in this intellectual tradition. Progress is originally conceived as the detachment from experience and as the opening of a wide horizon of expectations. But the more experience with possible progress is gained, the less expectation of actual progress there is. After a hundred and fifty years, the experience of autonomy, or so it seems, has cancelled the expectation of progress.

Between 1784 and 1944, the concept of progress had risen and declined. The thinking about progress had maintained a connecting thread, the notion of Enlightenment – or more broadly, of human autonomy. But in the course of observation and reflection, the emphasis had shifted from the *assumption* of autonomy to the *consequences* of autonomy. And whereas the former permitted a close connection between autonomy and progress, the latter questioned this connection – and increasingly so up to this historical moment.

Rereading the European Experience of Progress: Autonomy and Domination

At this point, the suspicion arises that proponents and critics of progress alike may have misinterpreted the European nineteenth-century experience. In the first step of reconstruction, we have looked at European thinkers of the nineteenth century observing the socio-political changes of their time. Intellectually, clearly, the European nineteenth century stood in the shadow of the Enlightenment and its commitment to autonomy. But in terms of practices and institutions much less so, as discussed in chapter 3. With the Vienna Congress of 1815, the revolutionary period was over for the time being. The revolutionary moments of 1830, 1848 and 1871 signal that the imaginary of autonomy was alive in Europe. But their occurrence and their suppression also demonstrate that European societies had not at all yet been transformed in the light of this imaginary. For reasons of this discrepancy between intellectual change and socio-political change, observers have misinterpreted the European nineteenth century as a history of progress based on autonomy and, accordingly, have exaggerated the consequences of autonomy.

The reasoning will proceed in two steps, as follows: first, it has been erroneously assumed that the era of autonomy had already begun. Consequently, secondly, identifiable structures of domination have been misread as a new kind of domination created by the commitment to autonomy. And as a consequence, to be discussed in the subsequent section, problems with progress that actually are related to the commitment to autonomy have largely been overlooked.

Thinkers of the late Enlightenment, such as Immanuel Kant, saw themselves as living at the dawn of a new era, the era of autonomy. They participated in the elaboration of a strong concept of progress, which was squarely based on autonomy, because they assumed that this era of autonomy had begun. We could say that future progress, based on the strong concept, was dependent on prior progress, namely the exit from immaturity. On a second look, though, we cannot be certain at all that the prior progress had indeed happened or was about to happen.

As we know, Kant speaks about *self-incurred* immaturity because it is not the lack of ability but the lack of audacity that lets human beings remain in a state of immaturity. He grants that lack of practice in making use of one's understanding entails current lack of ability. For that reason, learning is necessary and the societal exit from immaturity may take a long time. He also suggests that being guided by others may be a convenient state, so that not everyone will be immediately eager to exit from it and dare to self-determine their lives. These are some of the obstacles on the way to an era of autonomy.

But Kant does not consider the benefits that those who guide may obtain from telling others what to do, nor does he make a distinction between daring to think (*sapere aude*) and daring to act, when necessary, against immaturity that is not entirely self-incurred. In other words, he does not make a distinction between immaturity in general and formal, institutional domination. The difference is between becoming personally autonomous under conditions of formal equal freedom, on the one hand, and claiming one's autonomy by demanding equal freedom in situations where it does not exist on the other. The former is exit from self-incurred immaturity, the latter exit from domination.

Thus, for instance, Kant considers women as among those who find it more convenient to be guided than to make use of their own understanding. But he does not discuss the existing legal subjection to men at the time. He rightly claims for women equal capacity of understanding, but does not explore the fact that the prevailing view was that their capacity was not equal to the one of men, and that this inequality was sedimented in legal and institutional forms. As the French Revolution would demonstrate a few years later, the abolition of formal inequalities was on the political agenda during this period, with calls for equal rights and equal suffrage for women and men, the abolition of slavery and the abolition of serfdom. But slavery was formally abolished as late as the end of the nineteenth century in some countries; equal suffrage for men and women was rarely introduced in Europe before 1919, in France as late as after the Second World War; and equal rights often as late as the 1970s; only the abolition of serfdom proceeded at a quicker pace. While there was – and still is – self-incurred immaturity, there were also many forms of immaturity that cannot adequately be characterized as self-incurred. They did not mean primarily the acceptance of being guided by another, even though they may often have also entailed that. They meant the imposition of guidance that had to be obeyed, by means other than understanding, or at least also by means other than understanding. These situations are more precisely called situations of domination rather than, too generally, situations of immaturity.

If this can be accepted, the subsequent question is what impact the persistence of domination has for the strong concept of progress. The first consequence is the interruption of the conceptual connection between autonomy and progress that had been assumed in the strong concept. As we had seen, this connection was created by reason. Progress was sustained by the autonomous action of reason-endowed human beings. However, under conditions in which people are kept in immaturity through domination, and thus are not autonomous, one can no longer presuppose that an understanding of the situation will be developed that automatically entails progress. Secondly, and to some extent alternatively, a different substantive conception of progress would need to be developed for such situations. Under conditions of domination through formal inequality, every action that leads to the end of such domination will entail progress, at least progress of some kind, progress towards equality (as discussed in chapter 3). Such action would also be guided by some logic or dynamic: we may call it struggle for inclusion or struggle for recognition as equals. Achieved progress would mean exit from imposed immaturity and thus also greater autonomy. But it is no longer, as in the strong concept, the work of autonomous human beings itself that leads to progress. What is called progress here is rather the overcoming of heteronomy.

Returning to the European nineteenth century, one can say that forms of autonomy coexisted with forms of domination. Certain civil and political liberties and commercial freedom had been introduced. But many of the former were restricted to property-owning men, and the meaning of the latter depended very much on whether one had more to sell than one's labour power. In the light of the preceding reflection, the question would be how far one should look for the kind of progress that was expected due to the reason-based exercise of autonomy or for the other kind of progress – apparently logically prior, as one used to say in some Marxist debates – to be expected from the struggle for inclusion and recognition against domination.

We will come back to this question, but at this point of the conceptual reconstruction it is important to note that the thinking on progress of the time opted for a yet different interpretation. From Marx to Weber to Adorno and Horkheimer, primacy has been given to autonomy, but with the twist suggesting that the exercise of autonomy has historically created new forms of domination, to the point of undermining the possibility of autonomy.

As we have seen, this kind of analysis radicalized between the middle of the nineteenth and the middle of the twentieth century. Marx focused on commodification, but this entailed the emergence of a new class with the potential for creating the conditions for substantive autonomy. Weber concentrated on rationalization and could not find a systematic reason, only contingent possibilities, for further social change. Adorno and Horkheimer placed the emphasis on philosophical abstraction and saw the effects as totalizing, devoid of any angle for change.

Each of these perspectives speaks to and captures some aspects of the world they are about. In each case, however, one might also suspect that they considerably misread the historical evidence. Marxist thinking assumed that serfdom had become a fetter to the further development of the productive forces and needed to be abolished to pave the way for commodification. But would it not in many situations be more plausible to say that the abolition of serfdom impelled the elites to find other means to force the poor to work? If the latter is the adequate interpretation, then we have here a case of displacement of an issue as a consequence of achieved progress (as mentioned in chapter 3). Similarly, there may be a linkage between the protestant ethic and entrepreneurial spirit. But the modern-capitalist rationalization of the 'iron cage' form is much more associated with Taylorism and the conveyor belt, which stand in the continuation of attempts to control the workforce and have little to do with religious ethic. And though atomization and quantification through bureaucracy have been tools of totalitarian domination, it is difficult to agree that it was the socio-political consequences of abstraction that brought Hitler or Stalin to power.

These objections are not raised with a view to fully discarding the critiques of progress. Rather, they are meant to suggest that they help little in reconstructing the concept of progress for four reasons. First, they one-sidedly focused on the historical consequences of autonomy, thus making it difficult to retrieve this concept for a rethinking of progress, for which, though, it is necessary. Secondly, they have unduly neglected a different interpretation of progress in European post-Enlightenment history. Struggles against formal domination, namely, have by and large been successful in Europe, even though often only in the long run. They have created progress of some kind – as argued in the preceding chapter. But it is important to underline that they have predominantly been struggles for equal inclusion and recognition, against exclusion and misrecognition, not against commodification, rationalization or abstraction, even though negative consequences of these phenomena have often been felt and concerns about them voiced. One might even turn the perspective around: to some extent, commodification, rationalization and abstraction and quantification can be interpreted as measures taken by the elites to accommodate the successes of the struggles for inclusion and recognition, thus displacing the focus of socio-political struggle. As a consequence, thirdly, they have downplayed the possibility of considering progress – partial progress, to be sure, along some dimension, not comprehensive progress – to be achieved through domination, Marx being a significant exception. And finally, the critical interpretation of the consequences of autonomy has shifted attention away from the problems that emerge with progress under conditions that approach equal freedom. These problems were recognized in Enlightenment debate, but they were never frontally addressed for reasons that we need to now explore.

Progress between Personal Autonomy and Collective Autonomy

Autonomy is a problem for progress because it makes it extremely difficult to know and understand how social life will be arranged and organized, as we have seen before. If everyone is free to do what it pleases them to do, phenomena 'in the large' are nothing but the result of the actions of numerous human beings and their consequences. Endowed with reason, human beings give meanings to their actions, and their intentions are based on these meanings. This is what makes actions, in principle, intelligible for other human beings, as Weber underlined. But as the proverb has it, 'the road to hell is paved with good intentions'. We have no a priori ground to assume that the outcome of the actions of numerous free human beings is as intelligible as an individual action. And we have no ground either to assume that such outcome is as beneficial as the intended result of an individual action would be for the actor whenever the action is successful. That is why there is no straight line from autonomy to progress, as Kant already knew.

In other words, the commitment to autonomy introduces a high degree of uncertainty and contingency. As human beings live together with others, however, we nevertheless would like to know what the social result of the multiple exercise of autonomy is; and we would like to know in particular whether this outcome is beneficial for our lives. The authors we have looked at tried to reduce uncertainty and contingency while maintaining the commitment to autonomy. This ambition required them to make additional assumptions or observations.

As we have seen, the starting tension is conceived as one between *personal* autonomy and *unintended collective* outcomes of such autonomy. If we look at the political dimension of Enlightenment thought, though, the emphasis was not just on personal autonomy; it included a commitment to collective autonomy expressed as popular sovereignty or democracy. During the first half of the nineteenth century, it was often noted that the slogan of the French Revolution had been interpreted in a biased way, giving preference to individual over collective self-determination,

and the democratic impetus had been defeated in all repub-
lican debates of the time in Europe, North America and
South America. This bias and defeat are significant for the
concept of progress because actual processes of collective
self-determination could have been defined as the site at
which collective intentionality would be formed. And with
recourse to the human capacity for reason, a connection
between *collective* autonomy and progress could have been
formed that does not have to be too concerned about the
unintended consequences of the sum of individual actions.
We can read Jürgen Habermas's early investigation into the
emergence of the public sphere as a search for the elaboration
of such collective intentionality. But in a hyper-Kantian way,
he projected too much reason into the historical debates, as
later research showed. The experience of democracy being
absent, collective intentions cannot truly be detected.

Now we can read our authors in a different light. Having
identified the problem of unintended consequences of the
actions of a large number of autonomous individuals, but
being unable to access directly the possible outcome of collective autonomy, for lack of historical experience, they
needed to resort to substitutes. Kant – before and after the
French Revolution – aimed to detect the collective intention
in the reason applied by philosophers to history, a political
reason that would outweigh the play of human inclinations.
Half a century later, Marx envisaged positive collective
intentionality to be directly expressed by a rising universal
class, the proletariat, turning upside down, as he thought,
Hegel's notion of the state as the site of the universal. Another
half century later, Weber could not maintain either of these
hopes when analysing history. The 'iron cage' is without
spirit and movement; the only hope – but also danger – is
for the contingent eruption of old ideals or new prophets.
Another forty years on, Adorno and Horkheimer brought
this way of thinking to a conclusion. In their view, the

Enlightenment commitment to autonomy had been completely cancelled in the historical attempt at realizing it, thus a self-cancellation.

In the light of the whole tradition of approaching progress through the notion of autonomy, we can now ask what idea of autonomous agency is contained in these substitute solutions to the absence of actual collective agency. In Kant, there is implicitly some idea of political philosophers being able to accomplish the task of reading history from the angle of progress. But the question as to why those philosophers should have superior understanding is left open. In Marx, progressive agency clearly and explicitly resides in a social class, the proletariat, defined by its socio-juridical position. But here the very strong presupposition is that the commonality of social position creates common interest and, furthermore, that the expression of this interest of the working class will lead to the progress of humanity as a whole. Beyond his openness to contingency, one finds in Weber a trace of hope-providing agency in the charismatic personality. In Adorno, there is no agency; consolation – a term Kant already used – can only be found in the aesthetic realm.

Embarking on the notion that autonomy, given the context of its emergence as a guiding idea, undermined itself in the process of historical realization and led to entirely new forms of domination, critical theory failed to recognize how the contextual elaboration of a project of autonomy connected to actual forms of domination. A short conceptual discussion is needed before returning to the historical context.

As mentioned above, with the commitment to autonomy arises the question of certainty. Autonomy means giving oneself one's own law. Arguably, therefore, the idea of autonomy already contains a reference to mastery, namely to establish the law that henceforth is to guide one's own actions, or, in other words, to control the outcome of one's own actions. In this move, a tension is created: once there is a law to be followed, there is a limit to autonomy, to freedom. In the first instance, the temporality of human action is at the core of the matter: we may have freely established the law to follow at one moment, but at the next moment this law turns into a constraint. Cornelius Castoriadis referred to this tension as the relation between the instituting moment of social life – giving the law – and the instituted moment – facing the law that already exists. With this observation, we return to the double requirement of political progress, discussed above (in chapter 3), now rephrased in more general terms.

This relation appears paradoxical when the self that gives the law is always exactly the same as the one that obeys the law (as Kant knew; see clause 6 of *Idea*). This is what the term 'autonomy' suggests. In historical practice, though, these two 'entities' have been considered as standing in some separation from each other. Such separation was the historical way of establishing certainty under conditions of autonomy. For the nineteenth century, we can single out three types of separation. First, the law can emerge from, and be implemented by, an agency that knows what human beings *should* want for their life in common, rather than what they *actually* express. This agency was the more or less enlightened state that granted personal liberties but reserved the right to interfere with liberties in the name of the common good. Furthermore, it was possible to conceive of the main consequences of human autonomy as not being directed against one's fellow human beings, but against something or someone other. Thus, secondly, a main result of the unleashing of human autonomy was the increasing control of nature, and its exploitation, in what we have come to call the Industrial Revolution, allegedly for the good of all. And, thirdly, the exercise of autonomy as domination of others found its expression in European colonialism. For our purposes, it is important to underline that all three historical forms of domination – the enlightened liberal state, the Industrial Revolution and colonialism – have arisen in the context of increasing emphasis on autonomy in European politico-philosophical debate.

Across the nineteenth century, the prevailing perception was that some such combination of autonomy and domination was viable, and increasingly so. Debates about democracy, the realization of which would have moved the law-giving self closer to the law-abiding self, could be fended off and suppressed by the elites. The progress in the industrial transformation of the world was regularly celebrated at the World Fairs. And colonial domination reached its high point with the Berlin conference of 1884–5. Thus the actual relation between autonomy and control, far from the dilemma that it conceptually entailed, could be seen as evolving smoothly and progressively in a 'direction of development', even of progress from some point of view. It may not have had universal significance, but its global significance cannot be denied. Philosophies of history were at a loss to confirm its validity, but it was effectively validated through the power differential of the time. The increase of power and wealth of the European elites is the background against which what is discussed in terms of possibilities by Kant becomes the self-propelled dynamics of class struggle for Marx and the 'dwelling-places of steel' of 'victorious capitalism' for Weber. It was difficult to entirely rule out a pre-established direction of history.

Thus, in actual historical practice, it was not so much the undermining of autonomy in the process of its realization that shaped the nineteenth and early twentieth centuries, it was the combination of an increase of autonomy of the European elites with domination over nature, with domination over the majority of the European population and with colonial domination. From the elites' point of view, this was progress. From the point of view of critical theorists, it was not, but these theorists failed to recognize how progress had been derailed, not by the consequence of autonomy as such, but by the limited exercise of autonomy in combination with domination.

The absence of an experientially rich concept of collective autonomy and intentionality was crucial for this misreading. Paradoxically, this idea rose as a political concept while it withered away as a socio-philosophical concept. From the mid-nineteenth century, left-Hegelians were calling for over-coming liberalism with 'democratism'; and Tocqueville con-firmed democracy as the sign of the times. By the end of the century, the women's movement and the workers' movement had placed equal universal suffrage at the centre of their agenda as a precondition for realizing their substantive claims. By 1919, the idea of popular sovereignty had widely translated into the institutions of equal-suffrage competitive-party democracy. Against the often fierce opposition of the elites, the struggle for inclusion and recognition had success-fully supported the notion of developing institutions for collective self-determination. By the end of the First World War, these institutions, although not generally appreciated, appeared to be without alternative in Europe. At that time, though, their existence did not have any impact on the con-ceptualization of progress.

5

The Past Half Century

The Short-lived Return of Progress

By the middle of the twentieth century, it seemed that the concept of progress had been virtually abandoned. In his posthumously published 'Theses on the Philosophy of History' of 1940, interpreting a painting by Paul Klee, Walter Benjamin evokes the image of the angel of history. The angel is looking towards the past, 'one single catastrophe which keeps piling wreckage upon wreckage and hurls it in front of his feet', but is driven by a storm towards the future, 'to which his back is turned, while the pile of debris before him grows skyward'. 'This storm is what we call progress.' In this reading, what for more than a century had been called progress is seen as indeed having powerful agential capacity, driving history, which is not in the hands of human beings. This image draws on the strongest version of the concept of progress that we identified at the beginning, progress itself as an agent. But now this 'progress' has turned out to be an agent of destruction. A few years later, after the defeat of Nazism and the end of the Second World War, Karl Jaspers in 'The Origin and Goal of History' (1949) evokes a different image for a similar purpose: 'World history may look like a chaos of chance events – in its entirety like the swirling waters of a whirlpool. It goes on and on, from one muddle to another, from one disaster to another, with brief flashes of happiness, with islands that remain for a short time protected from the flood, till they too are submerged.'

These authors try to interpret the disastrous first half of the twentieth century, and they come to the conclusion that there is no hope for progress, or worse, in Benjamin's image, that the direction of history is one of increasing destruction. In the light of our earlier observations, however, we can read these philosophies of history much more contextually: what they signal is not the end of progress in general, but the end of European domination that engendered a particular kind of progress. This contextual reading finds confirmation by a second, comparative observation.

Apparently unperturbed by these European worries, the concept of progress re-emerged, even in a rather strong form but at a different site, in North America, reflecting the new hegemony in the world after the Second World War. Looking from a position of victory rather than defeat, US authors often expressed optimism about addressing and solving the problems that still remained, such as George Vannevar Bush in the 1945 report on science referred to in chapter 2. In academic terms, this optimism was most clearly and strongly expressed in the sociology of modernization, which is the philosophy of history attached to the functionalist theory of 'modern society', most prominently elaborated by Talcott Parsons.

This thinking drew on the Enlightenment commitment to freedom and reason but developed yet another interpretation of it. Progress was now possible on the basis of the institutionalization of autonomy in a functionally differentiated 'modern society'. It was suggested, on the one hand, that societies could be based on autonomy and initiative without the earlier unpredictability because freedom was exercised in well-defined institutional frames, and, on the other hand, that such initiative within these frames would produce further improvement through economic growth and scientific advance. This state had supposedly already been reached in some societies, most notably in the United States, and it was approached in some West European societies, while so-called Third World societies had embarked on a more long-term, but equally progressive, path of 'modernization and development'. Thus, the European despair of mid-century was swept away by the US enthusiasm of the 1960s. Even the last major political problem, the presence of Soviet socialism, would be solved by gradual processes of convergence driven by functional requirements.

But this enthusiasm proved to be short-lived: the protest movements of the 1960s, domestically as well as internationally, challenged the idea that an institutional situation had been reached in which smooth progress was possible. In turn, the failure of these movements to bring about significant political change in the West, jointly with the return of economic crises, triggered the declaration of the end of all grand narratives, another declaration of the end of progress. It was as if the history from 1789 to 1940 had repeated itself in fast motion between 1945 and 1979.

These observations suggest that we need to take a closer look at the recent past to understand what happened to progress. More precisely, we need to ask three questions about the past half century: first, we need to understand in new terms the socio-political constellation that was created between the end of the Second World War and the 1970s, also known as the *trente glorieuses*, the 'thirty glorious years', given that it had been misconceived as the functionally efficient institutionalization of freedom. Secondly, it remains an open question why intense critical activity by social movements that often understood themselves as 'progressive', between the 1960s and the 1980s, resulted in the withering away of progress. And this withering away of progress itself, thirdly, needs to be more closely scrutinized. Just as the return of progress after the Second World War was short-lived because it was based on an erroneous socio-political diagnosis, the disappearance of progress from the political agenda may be due to a misreading of recent occurrences – and may be short-lived as well.

Progress within Borders: Organized Modernity and Its Discontents

The global socio-political constellation around 1960 was widely perceived as relatively consolidated, as expressed in the then widespread use of the three-worlds image: a First World of liberal-democratic capitalism; a Second World of Soviet-style socialism; and a Third World of developing countries. This imagery was sociologically conceptualized from the First World point of view as itself having reached modernity, the status of 'modern society'; the Second World constituting a deliberate and organized deviation but with trends of convergence of those two worlds; and the Third World still needing to undergo processes of 'modernization and development'. These 'worlds', in turn, were composed of societies as unit elements, each of which, according to the dominant perception, had clearly demarcated borders and a state as a central institution with the effective power of monitoring the borders and organizing social life within the borders according to unified rules.

This imagery of orderliness and control also – in only apparent contradiction – extended to the expectations of progress. The stability of institutions was expected to channel change along predictable paths, making it possible to reap the benefits of progress without running the risks that come with entirely open horizons of the future. To grasp this ambiguous orientation towards the future, as both open and already known, it is useful to briefly return to the state of progress along the various dimensions where we left it at the end of chapters 2 and 3.

Progress of knowledge was expected to be 'endlessly' available for the benefit of society, but at the same time one had the closing of the last 'knowledge gaps' in view, thus ruling out any unpleasant surprises in the further pursuit of new knowledge. The lead projects that then captured the scientific-technological imagination, significantly, have since either been abandoned because of unsurpassable limits that made them unreasonable or have been seriously put into question because of the uncontrollable dangers that come with them: supersonic air travel; manned space exploration; nuclear energy. Economic progress was similarly to be channelled along predictable paths. Keynesian demand management, socialist planning and the development of a national industrial economy through import substitution policies were the strategies, as suited to one of each of the three 'worlds' by which economic growth could be reached without suffering the cyclical downturns that had marked the earlier history of capitalism. Applying these government techniques, economic progress would not only be steady but also lasting and good, thus providing the material background for also accomplishing social and political progress.

While epistemic and economic progress were meant to continue in a controlled way, social and political progress were thought to be completed and consolidated. For social progress, emphasis was placed on inclusion, to be reached with the extension of the welfare state regimes so as to protect all members of society against all conceivable risks, 'from the cradle to the grave', as Winston Churchill put it in 1943. In both Western Europe and socialist Europe, even though by different means, comprehensive social inclusion had been largely accomplished by the 1960s. In the United

States, it was announced as the core objective of the 'war on poverty', the key component of President Johnson's 'Great Society' programme. In Third World societies, similar social progress was at best distantly on the horizon. Inclusion within the First and Second Worlds relied on firm boundaries excluding the Third. Significantly, furthermore, social progress through welfare state measures meant a standardization of life-situations and, together with a male breadwinner full-employment economy, of life-courses. Individualization, therefore, was not a central criterion for social progress at the time. Political progress was conceived in a similar manner, as accomplished in some parts of the world and as accomplishable everywhere, provided that a restricted view on such progress was accepted. Accomplishment was defined as free and equal 'conventional' political participation, through which governments were elected that both had some degree of accountability towards the citizenry and were capable of designing and implementing policy programmes. This was reached in the First World, had found a particular interpretation in the Second and would be reached through political modernization in the Third. The restricted view entailed that the existing states should be the containers of political progress, and that within them a suitable balance was created between participation in collective self-determination and effective implementation of the common rules, in all situations of doubt priority being given to the latter over the former.

In the light of this brief characterization of the state of progress by dimension, one can recognize that the ambiguous orientation towards progress in the organized modernity of the post-Second World War period, as both open and known, expressed a novel relation between experience and expectations. The experiences of the first half of the twentieth century, in particular, had suggested that the widely open horizon of expectations permitted the rise of undesirable, even disastrous, experiences. In the terms developed above (chapter 4), these experiences had shown the limits of progress through domination, including the limits emerging from the risk that resistance to domination would lead to undesirable outcomes. The conclusion from those experiences was to narrow the horizon of expectations, through the institutions of organized modernity, without closing it entirely. Or, in other words, this was an attempt to select from the wide range of historically generated possibilities the limited number of those that appeared to be both functionally viable and normatively desirable.

With hindsight, one can see that this 'choice' – resulting from decisions of the early post-war political and economic elites – was only temporarily sustainable because of this ambiguity towards progress, which led to contradictory orientations. On the one hand, the progressive imaginary created two centuries earlier was now to be taken more seriously as a guide to socio-political practices. In public debate, the existing socio-political constellation was not presented as a power regime in principle equal to others in history, but as a socio-political order subject to normative justifications. Thus claims based on that imaginary – for individual liberty, collective self-determination, social justice – could not just be suppressed. They had to be addressed, in some way or other; and if they were not, pressure for change was likely to continue.

On the other hand, the particular form that this socio-political order took was shaped by the contingency of the moment. In this contingent context, significantly, the United States was the plausible site for developing the new view of progress for a number of reasons: it had been less directly a source of the disasters of the first half of the twentieth century. It had risen to be an economic power and transformed the economy into mass-consumption capitalism, thus had been successful in addressing the question of material needs. It had a reputation of greater political inclusion than European societies, despite the subjection of the native population and the discrimination of the African-American population, and thus appeared to have marked the direction of political progress. And up to this moment it had had a smaller role in colonial domination than Europe, presenting itself rather as one of the first post-colonial societies.

More generally, the contingency of the moment entailed that the conclusions drawn from the earlier experiences were to be implemented in the context of existing state boundaries, economic structures, gender relations and colonial domination. These contingent elements had a double meaning: they were there and thus unavoidable ingredients for the building of organized modernity; but they were not justified as such and often difficult to justify. They were used to build the institutions within which further progress was to occur in a channelled, controlled way; but they could turn out to be barriers to desirable progress and thus could be challenged by critique and protest.

This characterization provides a key to understanding the dismantling of organized modernity which proceeded at a rapid pace from the 1960s onwards. In the then so-called Third World, movements for national liberation called for decolonization and collective self-determination, these struggles reaching a high point around 1960. In the then so-called First World, the year 1968 marked a climax of worker and student contestation, often seen as the combination of political and cultural revolution, the former calling for intensification of political participation, the latter for widening the space for personal self-realization. In the then so-called Second World, protest called for both wider spaces of individual expression and for forms of collective self-determination that were not limited by the dominant interpretation of historical materialism, including self-determination as political collectivities that had not been recognized as such. In the wake of 1968, time-honoured issues were returned to the political agenda, with greater force and urgency, by the feminist movement and the ecological movement, calling for equality as well as recognition of difference and for critical reflection on the industrial transformation of the earth respectively. During the later twentieth century, new movements of the poor and excluded emerged in response to the consequences of global economic-financial restructuring, calling for social justice and inclusion. Where democracy had been abolished by military regimes, they merged with movements for the restoration of liberty and democracy. And where exclusion and oppression had a marked ethnic/racial component, contestations centred on political and cultural claims for collective self-determination.

Most of these movements can be called progressive because they advocated social and political progress by evoking the existing imaginary of such progress and by denouncing the restrictions that had been imposed on its realization. Some of these movements, furthermore, called for a rethinking of progress, criticizing the form in which progress had historically been conceived and supposedly realized. This is true for critics of epistemic-economic progress, pointing towards the increasing separation, and often contradiction, between actual epistemic and economic practices and the requirements for good answers to the epistemic and economic *problématiques*. Such critics often challenge the very mechanism of progress in these areas, as it was conceptualized historically. Some critics of social and political progress, in turn, called for a reconsideration of the contingencies that led to the present view of such progress, rather than of the principles. This is true for movements that challenge current polities and their borders as providing inadequate frameworks for collective self-determination. It is also true for protest that calls for rectification of historical injustice. While such calls may be interpreted as calls for social progress, they also insist that equal freedom in the present is an insufficient way to achieve such progress.

Protest and Progress at the End of Formal Domination

If the 1960s and the 1970s, to some extent also later years, were marked by strong protest movements, and if we have good reason to see these movements as having aimed for progress, to a considerable degree successfully, why then did progress wither away during this same period? To answer this question now in more detail, I want first to recall some earlier observations and then reconsider those in the light of this most recent socio-political transformation, the de-structuring of the organized modernity of the second post-war period.

At the outset, I suggested that socio-political change often occurs through reinterpretation of concepts that underpin the self-understanding of societies (chapter 1). Progress, then, is enhanced by reinterpretations that are suggested by the observation of persistent problems and the search for novel solutions to them. Social and political progress, in particular, is driven by protest against unsatisfactory situations: situations in which problems are addressed in ways that lack normative justification and/or functional efficiency (chapter 3). Across the nineteenth and much of the twentieth centuries, domination has been the prevailing engine of some kind of progress, whereas critique of domination has been a crucial way of reinterpreting progress. Equal freedom was not the historical starting point of the march of progress, as Enlightenment thought had postulated. Rather, it became the core component of the socio-political imaginary of progress, defining the goal of progress yet to be achieved. Rather than already effectively guiding prevailing practices, this imaginary inspired the resistance to those practices.

Prevailing practices in Europe, and later 'the West', brought progress about through domination: over nature, over other societies, and over sizeable parts of the population in their own societies (chapter 4).

Before the Second World War, these practices of domination kept being explicitly justified, even though they were increasingly contested. After the war, however, the mobilization of societies for the war and the justification of the war as a fight against illegitimate regimes changed the situation. The organized modernity of the post-war period meant to bring the prevailing practices in line with the socio-political imaginary. The societies of the First and Second Worlds claimed to be inclusive and egalitarian in social and political terms and committed to collective self-determination, even though in different understandings. The right to collective self-determination of the colonized societies was increasingly recognized, even though often after colonial wars and civil wars and by some colonial powers earlier than by others.

Looking again at the progressive movements that de-structured organized modernity, it is possible to compare them with earlier such movements. There are three main components to them: most similar to earlier protest, first, there were movements aimed at removing the remnants of formal domination. As such, they had proven to be enormously successful by the 1990s. The anti-colonial movement largely achieved its aim with the end of the last European colonial empire, the Portuguese one, in 1974 and with the end of apartheid in the early 1990s. Dictatorships and authoritarian regimes could no longer be maintained. The feminist movement secured full legal equality for women in many countries by the 1970s, in socialist countries even earlier, though not in most predominantly Islamic countries, an exception being Turkey. Civil rights movements, broadly understood, fought formal discrimination against ethnic and linguistic minorities, sexual orientation, and race, resulting in discrimination being outlawed, even though it often still exists in practice.

Second, the ecological movement aimed at ending the instrumental exploitation of nature and at returning the notion of economic progress to a substantive understanding of human material needs. In a sense, this is protest against domination, namely domination over nature, but not protest against domination by some groups of human beings over others. The current record of this kind of protest is ambiguous. It has had considerable success in bringing the ecological issue to the societal and political agenda. Nature-transforming activities are now in much greater need of justification than they were half a century ago, often even subject to institutional procedures of evaluation before being approved. At the same time, however, the scale of nature transformation has further increased: the industrialization of many 'emerging' economies far outweighs the de-industrialization of 'advanced' economies; and resource extraction techniques and processes go ever further in transforming nature. The prevailing notion at this moment, expressed in the debate about climate change, is that destruction proceeds at a higher speed than the attempts at halting or reversing destruction.

Thirdly, some protest aimed at reinterpreting the respective emphasis given to components of social and political progress. In societies where inclusion had largely been achieved but had led to the standardization of life-courses, individualization became a core concern. In societies where state capacity had been given priority over actual practices of collective self-determination, claims for intensifying political participation were made. This protest took a rather novel attitude to progress: it no longer aimed at overcoming formal domination, it aimed at redefining the social and political setting in substantive terms. It, too, was quite successful in one sense, but much less so in another: it succeeded

in undermining the dominant socio-political self-understanding within the varieties of organized modernity. But it
failed to elaborate a new hegemonic self-understanding that
is normatively superior to the preceding one, and which thus
marks progress.

In sum, the progressive movements that resembled most
those of the earlier past, those aiming at overcoming formal
domination, have largely been successful. Their success
explains the core components of the withering away of
progress: progress through domination was increasingly
limited by successful resistance to domination. And the more
resistance to domination marked progress, to the point of
nearly ending formal domination, the less central this kind
of progress would be to the future.

Due to the fact that this kind of progress was the one that
had been at the centre of critical thought, the ambivalent
notion of exhaustion/completion of historical progress could
arise. During the 1990s, specifically, there was a widespread
sense that critique had been disarmed in the ongoing socio-
political transformation, and it was difficult to see if and
how it could be reconstructed. At the same time, within
critical debate this apparent success was hardly ever perceived as a success, and this at least for some good reason:
new problems arose and old problems returned, namely the
ecological crisis and social injustice respectively, and the
political capacity to address them decreased, sometimes dramatically so.

A look at the South African situation is enlightening in
this respect. Under apartheid, South Africa had a vibrant
critical-intellectual debate focusing on the connection
between racial domination and the particular form of
South African capitalism. At the same time, it had a forceful
social and political movement for national liberation, the
core concern of which was the end of colonial domination
by claiming equal freedom and equal rights for all South

Africans. This domination was the target of critique, and its overcoming was what progress meant. With the end of apartheid, this aim was achieved. At the current moment, South African society faces numerous problems, most of which can be traced to the legacy of colonial domination: pronounced structures of social inequality due to apartheid segregation and injustice; an economy that is focused on resource extraction for a global market, rather than satisfying the needs of the South African population; and a public administration that was created to serve a minority but is inadequate for the needs of the majority in terms of education, health, transport infrastructure and so on. At the same time, there is a societal and political majority committed to an agenda of social transformation and to addressing these problems. But critical-intellectual debate is weak and disoriented, and there is considerable ambiguity about the kind of progress that is possible and how it can be attained, as well as pronounced doubt about whether any significant progress is possible at all. South Africa is not exceptional. Rather, it is exemplary because of the radical transformation it recently experienced by moving from violent formal domination to the commitment to personal and collective autonomy. It shows us that it is necessary to explore more insistently what progress means after the abolition of most institutional forms of domination. We need to understand how to translate the widely held idea of self-propelled progress as emerging from the Enlightenment combination of freedom and reason, once formal domination has been overcome, into a view of progress as a problem of collective self-determination, of collective agency.

For the remainder of this chapter, I want to insist that it is erroneous to overlook or denigrate the enormous progress that has been made in overcoming formal domination – factually erroneous because the achievements exist, but also politically erroneous because this view leads to an underestimation of normative forces in history. But I also want to demonstrate that the regress that has occurred was part of the same socio-political transformation that spelt the (near) end of formal domination and that it is even related to protests that aimed at progress. In other words, critique and protest provide reinterpretations that aim at normatively superior solutions, but they are not in control of the interpretations they provide and may end up supporting regress, the consequences of which outweigh the progressive achievements.

The Trap of Hegemonic Discourse: the Erasure of Space and Time

The protests that worked towards the dismantling of the conventions of organized modernity appeared in the form of rebellion against imposed constraints, in normative terms, or as consequences drawn from the insights into functional deficiency, in some instances as a combination of both criticisms. But they contained only a weak image of a constructive reinterpretation of modernity. The key elements of this image are all related to the aim of ending formal domination: the general idea of equal individual rights, such as in the women's movement, the civil rights movement in the United States or the struggle against apartheid; the idea of inclusive collective self-determination, or democracy, in liberation from colonial rule (including the particular case of South Africa) and from authoritarian rule such as in Southern Europe, East Asia and Latin America; and the ideas of freedom from particular constraints in the forms of commercial freedom, media freedom, freedom of movement and freedom for self-realization.

In the light of these objectives, much of the socio-political change that occurred can be described in terms of normative achievements, of progress of recognition, of freedom, of equality. This, precisely, is where the success of contestations can be located. When looking at the overall socio-political transformation, however, qualifications have to be added. Assessing recent change in terms of overcoming formal domination tends to overlook the fact that institutional components of organized modernity that were not as such containers of formal domination were dismantled in parallel. The normative assessment of these processes, however, is much more ambivalent, to say the least: the capacity of states to elaborate and implement public action diminished. In particular, the centrepiece of organized modernity, the steering of national economies, was abandoned. As a consequence, commercial and financial flows are increasingly beyond any control. More generally, institutionalized collective action was de-legitimized in the conceptual shift from 'government' to 'governance'. In parallel, the institutional frames for collective self-determination have been weakened, partly deliberately in favour of supranational or global cooperation and partly because of an alleged escape of socio-political phenomena from the view and grasp of political institutions.

Every major socio-political transformation entails the dismantling of existing institutions. But this dismantling is often accompanied by the building of new institutions, or by giving new purpose and meaning to existing institutional containers. The transformation of European societies from the middle of the nineteenth century to the early twentieth century, which was described above (in chapter 3) in terms of inclusion and recognition, is a strong example of the building of collective institutions to address problems that the earlier restricted liberal modernity of Europe had created. The contestations of organized modernity in the late twentieth century, in contrast, have often had the oppressive, exploitative or excluding nature of existing institutions as their target and have therefore been aiming at de-institutionalization in the first place. As an

unintended side effect, this orientation has tended to inca-
pacitate collective action on the one hand because specific
existing institutions are weakened, and on the other because
institutional rebuilding in general is de-legitimized in the
name of some generic concept of equal individual and collective freedom.

There was a moment in this exit from organized modernity, during the 1980s and early 1990s, when this weak
image of an ongoing reinterpretation of modernity gained
stronger contours. At this moment, much public political
philosophy suggested that a generalized commitment to individual freedom and to collective self-determination was
about to be globally and unproblematically implemented. It
would be accompanied and underpinned by an idea of economic freedom that suggested that constraints to economic
action are both freedom-limiting and dysfunctional for economic performance and thus need to be removed. These
politico-philosophical ideas translated into a political discourse about 'human rights and democracy' and an economic discourse about a strong return to market freedoms
and free trade, both in temporarily hegemonic positions.
Furthermore, these discourses found partial institutional
expression in various forms: in the abolishing of domestic
forms of economic regulation; in the lowering of international barriers to economic exchange; in the introduction of
the 'responsibility to protect' principle in international law
in tension with the principle of state sovereignty; in elements
of the internationalization of penal law; in the tendency to
identify public protest movements with an expression of collective self-determination, and so on.

Let me come back to the hare and the hedgehog. At the
beginning of the race, the male hedgehog described his *telos*
as a world of free human beings creating steady progress
through their interactions, and the hare started to run. When
much later the hedgehog's wife told the exhausted hare that

the race was over and won, the hare could not believe it, and was not able to understand. He could not tell the difference between the two hedgehogs. This is the problem that critical thinking about progress faces today: what is the difference between the promise of emancipation and equal freedom more than two centuries ago and the apparently widespread institutionalization of equal freedom today?

In other words, the question is what is wrong, if anything, with the discourse about 'human rights and democracy' and the idea that any elimination of constraints is an increase in freedom? The problem consists in the fact that there is clearly something right about these notions; they point to valid normative concerns, while at the same time that which is wrong with them is much more difficult to identify. The commitments to freedom, human rights and democracy present themselves as normatively uncontestable. The abolition of constraint on human action and of power over human beings appears self-justifying. This, however, is exactly the trap of hegemonic discourse: on the one hand, freedom and democracy are those basic normative concepts that one has to embrace. In this sense, they are indeed self-justifying. On the other hand, they are presented as the unsurpassable reference for all political debate, even though they are not, over-ruling all other considerations. Though valid and crucial, these concepts are not sufficient to guide political debate on their own. Rather, they open up further questions that need to be answered by drawing on other resources as well. To avoid falling into the trap – or, better, to get out of it, since much of current debate is trapped – we need to recall the insight that comprehensive evaluative concepts tend to be essentially contested (see chapter 1 above). They may be valid in a very general sense, but they do not lend themselves to application in the straightforward sense that specific action in the world can be derived from these concepts and equated with steps towards realizing them.

The history of these concepts is marked by a curious oscillation. As inalienable rights and popular sovereignty, they emerged with the Enlightenment and inspired the late-eighteenth-century revolutions. Political debate after the revolutions, though, devoted much energy to criticizing the concept of abstract freedom and prevailing notions about the constitution of modern polities. And in fact, socio-political transformations of the late nineteenth and early twentieth century reintroduced notions of social bonds and collective commitments. Current debate can usefully draw on the earlier period of conceptual critique and transformative practice. The retrieval of those debates, however, will be insufficient unless it is connected to the socio-political transformations of our time. Exactly with this objective in mind, I have tried to reconstruct the dominant self-understanding of the varieties of organized modernity after the Second World War, as well as the dynamics that led to their de-structuring. The public political philosophy that briefly became dominant afterwards needs to be interpreted as the spontaneous conceptual reflection of this de-structuring. Within sociological research, the idea arose that collective phenomena of all kinds – state, nation, class, society – were disintegrating, due to two dominant tendencies: globalization and individualization. Like the sociological theorem of globalization and individualization, the public-political discourse suggested that there was – and should be – little or nothing between the individual human being and the globe. Every social phenomenon that stood in between tended to be considered as having freedom-limiting effects. Significantly, the notion of democracy, which presupposes a specific decision-making collectivity and thus appears to stand necessarily in an intermediate position between the individual and the globe, tended to be redefined. Rather than referring to a concrete, historically given collectivity, processes of self-determination were, on the one side, related to social movements without institutional reference, and on the other side, projected on the global level as the coming cosmopolitan democracy. We can characterize this conceptual tendency as the *erasure of space*. In a second step, we can identify a similar tendency towards the *erasure of time*. The individual human beings in question are seen as free and equal, in particular as equally free. Thus, their life histories and experiences are no longer seen as giving them a particular position in the world from which they speak and act. And political orders are seen as associations of such individuals who enter into a social contract with each other, devoid of any particular history.

This is the image of a utopia. Progress is here the liberation from the determination by the space and time one was born in. The image can historically be found in theories of social contract from John Locke to Jean-Jacques Rousseau. But for these authors, and including their predecessor Thomas Hobbes, these were thought-experiments trying to find the bases on which peaceful human living together was possible at all (for Hobbes) and on which further improvements in the human condition would arise. In the outgoing twentieth century, in contrast, this image evoked imminent possibilities. It suggested the progress that was immediately on the horizon. This idea of liberation was then often sustained by a mode of critique that – in general, quite rightly – does not 'deduce from the form of what we are what it is impossible for us to do and to know; but [. . .] will separate out, from the contingency that has made us what we are, the possibility of no longer being, doing, or thinking what we are, do, or think'.

Such critique has been a major force for the dismantling of organized modernity from the 1960s onwards, be it in the struggle against colonial domination or in the northern '1968'. But it has also for too long and too often embarked on 'the affirmation or the empty dream of freedom', leading to misconceived 'projects that claim to be global or radical'.

These projects are those that aim at the erasure of time and space. They come in a variety of political forms: from the idea of individual enterprising selves relating to each other through self-regulating markets to the idea of individual human rights without any notion of the agency that guarantees these rights to the idea of cosmopolitan democracy devoid of an understanding of forms of political communication.

What, then, is to be done? In the words of the author already quoted on p. 121, Michel Foucault in 'What is Enlightenment?' (1984), the 'work done at the limits of ourselves must, on the one hand, open up a realm of historical inquiry and, on the other, put itself to the test of reality, of contemporary reality, both to grasp the points where change is possible and desirable, and to determine the precise form this change should take'. Without historical inquiry and reality test, the abstract reasoning about freedom and its consequences in terms of dismantling boundaries and forgetting experience becomes, rather than an ally, the opponent in the struggle over interpreting our present and identifying that progress which is both possible and desirable.

Preparing a Reality Test

Everything preceding in this essay can be read as a contribution to this historical and conceptual inquiry. The last step to take is to provide at least some elements for a test of current reality for possible and desirable progress.

At the current moment, the utopian image of progress as liberation from the constraints of historical time and lived space still exists, but it has lost plausibility and persuasiveness to a considerable degree. This is due to occurrences that have been interpreted as signs of its inadequacy, such as: a sequence of economic crises across the world; increasing concern about past injustice impacting on the present; the increased awareness of the consequences of human-induced climate change; regional crises of democracy; and lack of criteria for evaluating international conflicts. In the light of such occurrences, attempts at reconstruction are currently being made that are consciously situated in social space and acknowledge the historicity of human social life.

In some way, the events in Tehran in 1979, often referred to as the Iranian Revolution, are an early example of such reconstruction. As specific as the Iranian circumstances were, they can now be seen as an opening towards a broader understanding of political possibilities in the present, since then intensified not only by the strengthening of political Islam but also by 'emerging' novel political self-understandings from the variety of 'progressivist' political majorities in Latin America to the transformation-oriented post-apartheid polity in South Africa to post-communist China. The acceleration of European integration since the Maastricht Treaty, accompanied by intense debates about European self-understanding, is generally recognized as a major such attempt at regionally based world-interpretation – even though it is currently sometimes seen as on the verge of failing. More recently, the emergence of BRICS (Brazil, Russia, India, China and South Africa) entails a further proposal to reconstitute specific spatiality – some kind of global South – and temporality – rectification of past western (northern) domination. These observations suggest that one can analyse the present as an ongoing attempt at reinterpreting modernity, with again significant regional variations against the background of earlier experiences with modernity – in a context of greater connectedness that should not be misunderstood as actual globalization in the sense of erasing boundaries. This attempt is far from attaining a new consolidated form, but a key preparatory task for elaborating an adequate new concept of progress lies in identifying the main contours of these present processes of reinterpretation.

Against the background of the preceding observations, we can understand the past half century as the transformation of a globe composed of a set of consolidated regional, indeed: spatially defined, interpretations of modernity into a globe with de-structured social relations of highly variable extension and significance, but with the projection of a boundaryless setting populated by unattached individuals looming large. In very general terms, then, the current struggle over reinterpretations of modernity is characterized by two fundamental tensions:

- the tension between those who hold that the acceptance of the principle of equal freedom supports a view of the human being as holder of equal rights *in this time*, on the one side, and those who hold that the consequences of past experiences, not least experiences of oppression and injustice, weigh on the present and that there is a need for differential consideration of rights and normative claims, on the other. This is the question about the *temporal configuration of the present;*
- the tension between those who hold that *boundaries* limit the expression of autonomy, both political and economic, with negative normative and functional consequences, on the one side, and those who hold that boundaries are a precondition for the exercise of collective autonomy, which in turn is a necessity for the creation of spaces of personal freedom, on the other. This is the question about the *spatial configuration of the present.*

It is evident from the briefest of looks that there is intense struggle over the adequate resolution of these tensions in the contemporary world. The final task of this essay will be to see whether a notion of progress exists that can help in identifying the way towards the most adequate resolution.

6

Possible Progress Today

The Issues at Stake

The hegemonic discourse suggests that, conceptually, the *telos* of progress has been well defined as 'human rights and democracy'. And, historically, humankind only needs to overcome the last bastions of resistance to reach this end-point, variously located in religious fanaticism and misplaced attempts at collective imposition of a view of the good life. Today, the 'Islamic State' and 'Venezuela' are the markers of such impediments to fully accomplish progress in history, but yesterday they were 'Iran' and 'Cuba', and tomorrow they may have yet different names. More important than the moving targets of hegemonic thinking, however, is the fact that such impediments seem to re-emerge, regardless of the number of times and variety of circumstances under which the end of history has been proclaimed.[1] 'Mission

---

[1] Recalling Weber, these markers can be seen as referring to combinations of 'old ideals' and 'new prophets' that address the discontents with contemporary socio-political organization.

accomplished' is the most characteristic error when diagnosing progress in the march of freedom.

Hegemonic discourse blames its opponents for the error. It is wrong to expect, so the argument goes, that all problems will have been solved when 'human rights and democracy' are globally accepted. But there are, in this view, no superior principles of socio-political organization. And to expect to solve problems better by embracing illiberal commitments will only make things worse, so the reasoning continues. In the preceding chapter, however, I have tried to demonstrate that the attempt to detach the meaning of human rights and democracy from the spatio-temporal contexts in which they are to be realized paves the way for gross violations of the normative promises that these concepts entail. A project that presents itself as unsurpassably 'global and radical' turns out to be, in practice, the latest displacement of issues in power struggles of an increasingly global nature.

More than any preceding one, this latest displacement requires us to rethink the very concept of progress for our time. In earlier periods, the suggestion that the contemporary era was committed to equal freedom could be denounced by pointing to the evident absence of equality and freedom in some or other respect. Thus future progress could be defined as overcoming formal domination, and all possible progress would be accomplished once equal freedom for all was achieved. Today, formal domination is certainly not entirely overcome, nor equal freedom entirely achieved, but past progress in these respects has been so significant that it is no longer credible that considerable future progress along similar lines remains to be made. This explains the exhaustion of progress. But, in conclusion, I now want to show that it is only progress of one kind that can no longer guide us, and that progress of another kind is both necessary and possible.

The key to this demonstration is the reality test announced earlier. We need to analyse current socio-political reality in the light of the effects of the hegemonic discourse – its actual effects in as far as it has guided recent socio-political change, and its potential future effects were it to remain hegemonic. Concretely, this analysis can start out from the promise that the abstract concepts of individual and collective freedom can actually be realized in the ongoing processes of 'globalization' and 'individualization'. More radically than at any earlier moment, some versions of the hegemonic discourse have implied that the globe today can be inhabited by free individuals relating to each other as equals and interacting without boundaries and intermediaries. This is what we have referred to above as the erasure of time and space.[2]

If one accepted the hegemonic discourse, there would still be a clear orientation for progress, as little as it may be compared to past progress. All still existing boundaries and institutions that limit the movement of human beings in space would need to be dismantled. And all attachments of human beings that stem from their past would need to be considered insignificant for the present. This would mean the true realization of equal freedom. If, however, as

---

[2]Conceptually, that which is here called the erasure of space and time can be traced back to the philosophy of the Enlightenment with its notion of abstract individual freedom. Already during the nineteenth century, the dynamics of social transformation was often described in similar terms, most strongly in Karl Marx and Friedrich Engels's *Communist Manifesto*, but also in later classical sociology. Thus the themes and concepts as such are not new. But they gain their particular significance from the current context of 'globalization', sometimes indeed defined as 'time-space compression'.

indicated earlier, we have reason to assume that to embark entirely in this direction is not desirable, we need to identify in more detail and more concretely where future progress can be sought and the means by which it can be attained.

This work can start by turning the question around: if dismantling of boundaries is not always advisable, what are the spatial structures that are desirable? If the erasure of the past does not necessarily aid in truly achieving equal freedom, what is the significance of the past for the present? We will call what follows an attempt at reconstituting meaningful spatiality and historical temporality. Four preliminary remarks may be needed: first, this is work at *re*constitution because the hegemonic discourse has cast considerable doubt on the usefulness of social structures of time and space, and its force has weakened many of them in practice. Thus current reconstitution happens after quite some work at erasure. Second, reconstitution should not be understood as attempting to return to earlier spatio-temporal constellations – because a straight return is not possible, but also because it may not be desirable. Thirdly, what follows are not just conceptual reflections accompanied by speculations. Such work at reconstitution is currently going on in manifold forms in many parts of the globe. But, finally, one cannot presuppose that any work at spatio-temporal reconstitution marks progress. These observations are only the preliminary to identifying kinds of possible progress in the second part of this chapter.

The Reconstitution of Historical Temporality

The question of temporality presents itself today as the tension between a political self-understanding erected on abstract and 'presentist' concepts of the individual and the collectivity, on the one hand, and the widespread experience of human beings as living under, or having only recently emerged from, conditions of domination and injustice that keep making themselves felt in the present on the other. In the former view, the present dominates over the past. Whatever conflictive relations may have existed in the past, those conflicts need to be 'come to terms with' and the past 'settled', put to rest. The latter view, in contrast, suggests that there is a present significance of the past which needs to be taken into account in current action. Equal freedom in the present, in this view, means the perpetuation of past domination in the form of the current consequences of this domination. One can distinguish two central issues in current debates over the interpretation of temporality: (1) ways of dealing with historical social injustice, understood in terms of social progress; and (2) ways of dealing with the current consequences of the instrumental transformation of the earth in the pursuit of epistemic-economic progress.

1 The significance of historical injustice for the self-understanding of contemporary societies begins to be widely recognized, much beyond the so-called 'divided societies' to whom only the need for 'settling the past' was normally ascribed. After the dismantling of organized modernity, numerous polities reconstituted themselves by some break with the past – of colonial domination, dictatorship, authoritarianism, apartheid, Soviet-style socialism – and based their self-understanding on this rupture. Post-apartheid South Africa is particularly significant in this respect because the new polity is centrally based on the recognition of past injustice and the need for corrective action. It also embarked on a revelatory public exposition

of past violence, in contrast to the silence that was often agreed between the post-transition elites elsewhere. However, South Africa was an exception, or maybe an avant-garde, in this respect. Much more widespread had been the notion that a 'settling of the past' with a view to enhancing capacity for action in the future was necessary, such as in the 'negotiated transitions' in Spain, Chile and Argentina. Accordingly, a political theory became suitable that was based on the abstract freedom of individuals who are held to reason from behind a 'veil of ignorance' (John Rawls) and privatize their past experiences. However, injustice persists in social relations and institutions, shaping the outcome of present action, even though the actual harmful deeds were committed in the – more or less distant – past. In more recent years, it has been increasingly recognized that existing democratic polities are historically constituted and that their constituent moments keep shaping the societal self-understandings, sometimes even provide their *raison d'être*. This is evident, for instance, in the constitutional commitment to remedy past injustice in Brazil and South Africa, but also in the re-emerging debates in Spain, Chile, Argentina and elsewhere.

More generally, it is often precisely the introduction of equal legal freedom that lets the topic of the current consequence of past injustice emerge, both in intra-polity and in global settings. The end of formal domination necessarily spells the end of the critique of formal domination. However, the end of formal domination does not mean the end of inequality in numerous other respects beyond rights. Thus the reasons for current inequality – and thus, arguably, injustice in the present – are being sought in the present consequences of past injustice. Gender equality and the lasting effects of colonial domination are the themes of the most widely diffused such debates.

The articulation between domestic and global debates becomes particularly visible with regard to the effects of colonial domination. In America, both North and South, these effects, including slavery, are addressed in predominantly domestic contexts, in terms of the claims for cultural and other rights for the indigenous population and for affirmative action for the African-American population. At the same time, a compelling argument can be made that the structures of *global* social inequality today are to a significant degree a legacy of colonial or neo-colonial domination. Social inequality, though, is today predominantly measured through the Gini coefficient based on *national* statistics. Thus the rectification of past global social injustice, aimed at further social progress, faces a triple problem of interpretation: the elaboration of a case for attributing current unjustified inequality to past actions; the measurement of the degree of injustice and, thus, the amount of remedial action that is appropriate; and the identification of actors that can develop and implement remedial action.

2 The global dimension is immediately central with regard to the contemporary consequences of the instrumental transformation of the earth. Industrialism in all its aspects – mass production, mass consumption, transport infrastructure – is the main cause of climate change and its likely consequences in terms of deteriorating living conditions on the earth. It was developed by the early industrial powers in north-western Europe and later North America for their own benefit, but dependent on the creation of an Atlantic division of labour involving African labour and American soil in the European 'take-off' of industrialism. Without climate risk, this constellation could largely be analysed in politico-economic terms, underlining not least that the recent industrial dislocations are an important cause for economic growth in the so-called 'emerging'

societies, and the dangers to the environment are a 'price to pay' for this growth. In other words, the instrumental transformation of the earth is not 'as such' a temporal issue. However, the current impasse in dealing with it is strongly related to past domination and appropriation. Across the nineteenth and much of the twentieth centuries, 'modernist' and colonial discourse had relegated the colonized societies to a 'not yet', had denied them coevalness in the present and, thus, economic progress as then defined, underlining immaturity to be overcome by education or the missing institutional preconditions for an industrial take-off. This 'backwardness' (Gerschenkron, 1962), however, was induced by the relation of domination between colonizers and colonized, as dependency theory would later underline. Currently, societies in the world relate to each other as formally equal. And it is as equals, supposedly, that they try to find a solution to the pressing issue of climate change. Given the urgency, there is a strong inclination in the current debate to deny the 'emerging' societies significant increases in resource extraction and consumption for the sake of keeping the earth inhabitable. This debate, though, operates against the historical background that the benefits of industrialism were historically reaped by the 'advanced' societies, a fact that is insufficiently acknowledged by current formal equality.

The Reconstitution of Meaningful Spatiality

From the so-called discovery of America onwards, the emergence of global consciousness has led to attempts at neatly dividing up the space on the planet, from the treaty of Tordesillas in 1494 to the 'scramble for Africa' in the nineteenth century. Beyond power-political considerations, these and other similar attempts often combined normative and presumed functional aspects in the light of a coexisting variety of different world-interpretations. Thus, the principle *cuius regio, eius religio* assumed that only people with similar fundamental beliefs could live peacefully together and be well governed, a supposed insight from the European religious wars. Similarly, the principle of popular sovereignty was often seen as requiring a 'people' to share the same space, justifying wars over territory, 'ethnic cleansing' and forced relocations. During the nineteenth century, political progress was seen as entailing the adequate setting of boundaries.

Recently, in contrast, it was widely assumed that globalization and individualization would make the alleged spatial preconditions of organized social life irrelevant. Migration made societies more diverse, and liberal multiculturalism was an intellectual response, suggesting that such diversity within a space does not need to be problematic. By now, however, it is clear that the question towards which spatial separation was historically seen as the answer does not so easily go away. The question keeps addressing today both (1) the persistent variety of world-interpretations and (2) the reach of collective self-determination, the two key issues that underpinned the historical case for separation.

1 Not least since the rise of political Islam, world-views and values are taken more seriously again; and 'alternative modernities' (Dilip Gaonkar) are discussed in terms of world-interpretations rather than social interest. The debate about the Christian roots of Europe, as arising over the preamble to the constitutional treaty of the European Union; Samuel Huntington's view of coexisting different

civilizations; or the reasoning of Islamic fundamentalists that their struggle is justified by the invasion of Islamic territory by western values are expressions of the same issue: on the one hand, meaning-providing frameworks, sometimes related to religion or political ideology and sometimes described as 'cultural', appear as specific and particular but, on the other hand, the degree of proximity, connectedness and interaction in the contemporary global context requires engagement with the other, rather than separation from them.

2 Modern democracy and modern capitalism have coexisted in a coherently articulated form in parts of the world only and during short periods, mostly the decades after the Second World War. More profoundly, there is a general tension between the expansionist dynamics of a capitalist economy and the necessary stability of democratic political forms, also in spatial terms. The current European situation, in which the incapacity of governments to address fiscal deficits and unemployment leads to citizen disaffection, is often diagnosed as a 'crisis of democratic capitalism' (Streeck 2011) from which there is no return. However, the view that there is a globalized, spaceless economic arrangement that generally limits and determines the range of political options is misleading. It underestimates the existing variety of relations between democracy and capitalism: the European situation is considerably different from the one in the United States, on the one hand, and from the ones in Russia and China on the other. Significantly, the current constellation also witnesses intensifications of political participation and democracy, such as in many Latin American countries, South Africa and India. These different regional institutional constellations are supported by different interpretations of the relation between collective self-determination and the satisfaction of material needs, or in the terms proposed above, of the

connection, or not, between political progress and economic progress.[3]

This brief characterization of the current global sociopolitical constellation in terms of responses to the erasure of

[3] State boundaries have been discussed from various angles in the preceding pages, starting with the exploration of social and political progress in chapter 3. At this point, the ambivalence of boundaries becomes fully clear: I defend here the need for meaningful spatial structures in general and for the boundedness of collective self-determination in particular. This should not make us overlook, however, that boundaries are also expressions of unjustifiable injustice, perpetuating the consequences of past power and domination into the present. We live today, for instance, with a global division of social labour, which according to classical ideas enhances global wealth creation, but we reject a notion of global ('organic') solidarity that should follow from such division. In a broad sense, it is unjust to exploit Nigerian oil reserves for the benefit of European companies and consumers while denying Nigerian citizens access to European territory. More specifically, global interconnectedness is today of such a kind that no absolutely unilateral right to determine access to a political space should be upheld, in contrast to European Union practices in particular with regard to African migrants. The notion that today's states are in relations of equality towards each other is an erasure of historical time analogous to the fiction of the abstract individual. That this reasoning is valid while at the same time the reasoning in favour of bounded political spaces should also be maintained demonstrates the need for nuanced interpretation, to be discussed further below. The example, furthermore, points to ambiguities in – possibly limits of – the very definition of formal domination as proposed here: on the one hand, one can suggest that decolonization ended the formal domination of the colonizers over the colonized. On the other hand, citizenship can be seen as constituting categories of persons, and thus the holding of a passport that permits access to 'precious' social spaces can be seen as formal domination over those who hold other passports.

time and space should have achieved the following: it should have shown, first, that significant – in some respects, dramatic and urgent – problems exist and tend to aggravate in a world apparently governed by the commitment to equal freedom. Some of these problems are indeed the consequence of solutions to earlier problems: what was once perceived as progress can no longer be seen as progress today. Second, it should also have demonstrated that the principle of equal legal freedom does not provide a guide for further progress, for better solutions to these problems. All of the four key issues escape from the reach of any straightforward application of the principle of equal freedom. Thirdly, however, it is not immediately evident either in which other direction one should search for further progress. While the solution to the problems can be formulated in general terms – globally extended and historically sensitive social justice; a sustainable engagement with the earth; peaceful and mutually enriching coexistence of diverse world-interpretations; democratic embedding of economic practices – the ways in which such solutions can be approached are much less clear. In other words, there is no easily visible 'mechanism' for reaching further progress today. For these reasons, our search to identify possible progress today will proceed in the next step by briefly reassessing the findings on the historical mechanisms for progress in the light of the current global sociopolitical constellation.

Progress Under Conditions of Autonomy: Agency and Critique

Our earlier reconstruction (in chapter 4) had shown that the most reliable 'mechanism' for progress until the middle of the twentieth century had been formal domination. For this reason, it is worth, first, exploring whether this source might be mobilized again in the present. Normative objections will obviously be raised: the imposition of the will of some on others does not align with the commitment to equal freedom. However, we have also encountered the argument that benefits in the progress of knowledge and in the satisfaction of needs might outweigh lack of progress in personal and collective self-realization. There may be something like benign domination, imposed on others for their supposed benefit and for the common good, and further enabled by the unwillingness to exit from immaturity, as diagnosed by Kant. After all, this is how European elites liked to see their role in colonial domination, and similarly the way in which the US elites tended to characterize their hegemony during the short period in which they carried the torch of the strong belief in progress. Whether one accepts this reasoning or not, I want to suggest that it has become unjustifiable today in this form and that it is unlikely that we will witness a return to a situation in which one pre-defined group of people asserts its domination over others whom it places deliberately into a situation of heteronomy.[4]

This does not mean, however, that reasoning has ceased to exist that calls for limitations of autonomy in the name of progress. The most common one is the appeal to a form of knowledge that demands certain behaviours and limits choices. Today, maybe most significantly, we live under the hegemony of liberal-capitalist thinking that makes claims to expertise, often implying the subordination of collective self-determination under requirements for economic progress. Similarly, though more reluctantly, it is sometimes argued that our scientific knowledge about climate change demands

---

[4]The main remaining exception today is the domination of parents over children, or generally of specially authorized persons over persons with limited capacity for autonomy. Even in those situations, it is observable that the need for justification has increased over the past half century.

the adoption of certain measures, whether people want them or not. In the terminology adopted at the outset, though, this is not formal domination. It is a kind of domination that needs to be identified by other means, to be explored below, than the standard approach to emancipation and recognition.

Secondly, the tension between autonomy and certainty, which had already been diagnosed by Kant and was a key challenge to expectations of progress for Burke, persists. Arguably, it has increased considerably. The commitment to individual autonomy is much more widespread than two centuries ago. At the same time, the phenomena that exist 'in the large' appear to have increased in dimension and significance and have ever more acquired a dynamics beyond control – this is what is often implied by the use of the term 'globalization'. As a consequence, a view of the world has become more widespread in which that which exists 'in the large' is nothing but the unintended aggregate of a large number of individual decisions and actions. If we had to submit to this view, we should no longer expect progress. Unlike Condorcet thought, there is no convincing a priori reason to assume that a large number of decisions by isolated human beings yields beneficial results in general, and even less that it does so in a persistent way.

Thirdly, to sustain an idea of progress under conditions of autonomy, therefore, one would need to identify a way of constructing collective intentionality, adequate for the current situation, as a response to the lack of certainty and control over the outcome of uncoordinated actions. To address this issue, there is little one can draw on in the history of social and political thought. The possibility of sustaining the achievement of positive collective outcomes by conceptual presupposition, on the model of Kant's philosophical reason or Marx's universal class, seems today even more remote than Weber in his time suspected.

But there is one exception: a notion of democracy as collective autonomy. The idea that free human beings get together to deliberate about the best ways to organize their living together and to address problems they face in common effectively provides an answer to the question of how phenomena 'in the large' with positive normative contents can come into existence. And, after all, the commitment to collective self-determination, to democracy, has become much more widespread in the course of the twentieth century, in particular its second half. Thus this answer can well be seen as the one appropriate for our time. However, this answer shifts the burden of proof onto the ways in which, and the conditions under which, human beings arrive at collectively agreed decisions. While we may hope for progress today through collective self-determination, we need to inquire in more detail about the prospects for realizing this potential.

Pending the outcome of this inquiry, fourthly, we can already state that critique has become both more necessary and more difficult. Critique works with a difference between reality and possibility. It can do so by demonstrating that prevailing practices do not accomplish what they claim to accomplish. Or it can do so, more radically, by arguing that prevailing practices are not aiming at that which they should be aiming at. For both reformist and radical critique, it is useful to have a clear measure for demonstrating the difference between reality and possibility, as well as a reasoning about why prevailing practices systematically deviate from that which is both possible and desirable. Today, critique is more necessary because the gap between that which is collectively desirable and that which is likely to happen as the uncoordinated outcome of actions has grown very wide. But it is more difficult because there is, after the end of formal domination, neither a clear measure of the difference between the possible and the real, nor a straightforward reasoning why more is possible than that which is real. If it is not formal domination that prevents progress from occurring, then maybe we already have all that we can have; or at least there are no systematic, only contingent, reasons why humankind does not progress as much as it could.

This means that, to use neo-Marxist terminology, we can no longer straightforwardly 'derive' practical conclusions, which show the way ahead towards progress, from an expert critique and denunciation of power and domination. As little as one can expect decisive action to emerge from philosophical reason or a universal class, as little can one expect the adequate analysis of the situation to emerge from the expertise monopoly of the critic. Instead, in analogy with the question of collective agency, the emphasis needs to be put on the critical capacity of human beings themselves, enabling them to arrive at the appropriate interpretation of their condition.

Under current conditions, in sum, we should not expect future progress from resistance to formal domination and from adding up the actions of autonomous individuals. In turn, there is the prospect of considerable progress through democratic collective agency applied to the key problems of our time and through the work of critical interpretation pursued by the actors themselves.

Possible Progress (1): Building Democratic Agency

To insist on the building of democratic collective agency as a core component of future progress may seem superfluous, given that the past half century can be seen as much marked by 'democratization' as by the end of formal domination. Should the building of democratic agency not be seen as past progress rather than future progress? Without doubt, there is past political progress in the sense that people who had been denied the right to political participation have conquered it, most clearly in the cases of colonial domination, apartheid and dictatorships and authoritarian regimes. However, this achievement is better understood as a component of the end of formal domination, namely of those who acted politically over those who were denied this right. Lifting the formal restrictions to political participation does not mean that collective self-determination has been reached. The latter has much higher presuppositions than the former. We need to take a closer look.

In recent years, protest movements in so-called consolidated democracies, such as Spain and the United States, have called for 'real democracy now'. This is a rather confusing slogan. There can be little doubt that Spain and the United States have democratic institutions and procedures, based on free and equal universal suffrage, supported by freedom of expression and enacted through competing parties. Furthermore, such democracies are also open to change. Those who suggested that structural asymmetries would for ever prevent an African-American candidate from being elected president of the United States or a radical opposition from having electoral success have been contradicted by Barack Obama's election in the United States and Syriza forming the government in Greece. That 'progressive' social movements can gain institutional political power was impressively demonstrated even earlier by the African National Congress in South Africa or the Workers' Party in Brazil. To deny 'reality' to existing democracy means diminishing past progress. It also undermines our capacity for distinguishing between different political situations, such as Spain or South Africa in 1970 from Spain or South Africa today.

Nevertheless, there is something valid about the concern that this slogan expresses, namely that collective self-determination is found wanting despite the fact that procedures for self-determination exist. This situation results today from three layers of transformation of democracy over the past half century. First, as mentioned earlier (chapter 3), currently existing institutions had been set up with a view to discouraging citizen participation beyond elections. Thus a divide between the citizenry and the 'political class' was created, which limited the power of the former so as to merely select sections of the latter for political office. The determination of political choices was left to communication within the political class. More recently, triggered by the 'legitimacy problems' arising during the 1970s, the political elites abandoned the project of setting societal priorities. Rather than being the site where the collective will was formulated and implemented through 'government', the state resorted to mere 'governance', conceived as moderation between societal actors. This latter change was accompanied by the growing interdependence of societies and their openness to outside influences. As a result, even when they are willing to do so, governments have today much less power to implement political choices than they used to have. This is most obvious with regard to the decreasing capacity to steer the national economy, but it applies also to other policy areas.

Against this background, the direction of political progress is rather clear. The building of democratic agency would reconnect the idea of progress to a notion of collective autonomy that answers the question of how autonomous human beings can act together to find the adequate solutions for their living together. Such democratic agency would be based on intense participation in the identification of key problems and the ways to resolve them, rather than on the numerical summing up of numerous individual decisions in elections and opinion polls. It would emphasize the legitimacy of collective choices developed through such participation, not against personal freedom, but against the idea of the primacy of individual autonomy. And it would develop cooperative ways of dealing with interdependence between societies and polities, in particular with regard to issues of global concern such as climate change and the regulation of financial flows.

It may seem surprising that existing democracies are so far away from the desirable state portrayed here. After all, collective self-determination and democracy had been declared the guiding ideas of politics after the First World War, and they have increasingly been institutionalized after the Second World War. Reaching this point, though, we find that the era of 'democratization' is the one, paradoxically, in which the will of the citizens has few chances to find adequate expression and even fewer to be implemented as political choice. Hegemonic as a procedural notion, democracy is increasingly emptied of substance today. Exploring the reasons why this is so, we approach the second type of progress that is both necessary and possible in our time.

Possible Progress (2): Overcoming New Kinds of Domination

Faced with high levels of political mobilization after the First World War, elites first abolished democracy in many countries and then reorganized it in the way described above, limited to electoral participation and elite selection. Faced again with rising demands at the end of the 1960s, they restricted the range of policy choices by making economies and societies more interdependent, thus no longer subject to spatially limited collective self-determination, and reducing the meaning of government to providing incentives for individual, group or corporate activity, employing techniques of new public management. In the terms introduced earlier, we witnessed here, first, a situation of formal domination, namely exclusion from political participation, which was successfully overcome by resistance. Subsequently, though, the issue is displaced repeatedly, and collective self-determination in the full sense of the term is not reached, despite equal freedom to participate politically. This new situation is one that is devoid of formal domination but needs to be understood nevertheless as some kind of domination.

What is domination after the end of formal domination? Rather than trying to improve on the provisional definition given above (in chapter 1), it is fruitful to return to the process that leads from formal domination to new kinds of domination (as tentatively sketched in chapter 3). As underlined before, the resistance to formal domination was one of the most powerful forces of progress in history. It defeated the privileges of elites by insisting on normative claims, at the core of which is equal freedom, across all walks of life. Often after long and protracted struggles, frequently including violence, the elites gave in. Equal freedom became more and more the organizing principle of socio-political organization. Historically, the granting of equal freedom rarely occurred on the basis of a new consensus, but was an elite concession, often demonstrably granted under siege by the contestants rather than out of normative conviction. And the elites did not disappear with the end of formal domination. They tried to displace the terrain of struggle, aiming at maintaining their privileges in forms that could not be subjected to the critique of formal domination.

Historically, this displacement often entailed the shift from one kind of formal domination – the one that was effectively resisted – to another, rather than the end of formal domination. The social and political progress of inclusion and recognition in Europe and North America during the second half of the nineteenth and the first half of the twentieth century forced the elites to intensify the domination over other societies – through colonialism – and over nature – through industrialization. The intensification of industrial work during the twentieth century, pioneered by F. W.

Taylor's 'scientific management', can be seen as a similar step within 'northern' societies after the workers' movement had achieved the improvement of working conditions, higher wages and the societal commitment to social security. In this case, the formal domination is exercised by the owners of the means of production over those who have only their labour power to sell.[5]

Such displacements were characteristic of the era in which progress was achieved through formal domination and the resistance to such domination. In the course of such progress, a direction of history became visible in the sense that fewer and fewer kinds of formal domination remained to which issues could be displaced. There are hardly any colonial societies left, no unfree others who can be formally dominated. The industrial transformation of the earth arguably has reached its limits; thus, intensification of the domination of nature is less an option (a question to be returned to in a moment). And the denial of formal equal freedom is hardly justifiable any longer. Therefore, the only displacement possible is towards new kinds of domination – domination that no longer implies a formal and justified hierarchy of one category of persons over others.

The brief sketch of transformations of democracy above gives an example. Formal political domination exists where categories of persons are excluded from participating in determining the rules of socio-political organization: under

---

[5]With the distinction between 'formal' and 'real subsumption' of labour under capital, Marx referred to what is here called displacement for the particular case of capital–labour relations. The term displacement widens the meaning to general aspects of conflicts between normative claims and entrenched interests and underlines the fact that the phenomenon is not due to any 'capital logic', but often is a response to achieved progress in the resistance to domination.

conditions of restricted suffrage or colonial domination, for instance. Once free and equal suffrage is granted, formal political domination ceases to exist, but not political domination as such. Similar observations can be made in other realms: once men and woman have equal rights, formal gender domination disappears, but not male domination over women in general. The granting of equal rights similarly does not make ethnic and racial discrimination disappear, but the dominating group loses an important tool to impose itself over others. The managerial capitalism that spreads during the twentieth century tends to abolish the core distinction between owners of capital and owners of labour power that informed the most significant critiques of capitalist domination. But it does not make power differentials between economic agents disappear.

Two questions emerge from these observations. First, if current domination is no longer – or much less than before – based on formal distinctions between the dominating and the dominated, what is it based on? And subsequently, second, how does critique of domination operate when domination is no longer formal?

The first question can be answered with reference to my preceding analysis of the work of hegemonic discourse: it is based on the erasure of time and space as new forms of displacement. Under conditions of formal equal freedom, effective domination is today largely based on past formal privilege. This can be inherited economic capital in the classical sense. In the South, this is very often land ownership, which makes the question of land reform central for reducing inequalities. In the United States, the cost of winning an election makes running successfully for office a privilege of the few, thus showing how historically built economic disparities undermine equality of political rights. But this can also be cultural or social capital in terms of educational background and social networks, which privileges some members of societies over others regardless of individual merit. When present equal freedom means that distinctions of the past cannot be evoked for organizing current practices, this erasure of historical time creates situations of domination by perpetuating past injustice.

The erasure of space works in two ways to sustain or create domination. On the one hand, struggle against domination requires collective action, and, for a collectivity to organize itself, boundaries are required. Historically, states have marked the space in which collectivities were formed that could formulate normative claims and achieve social and political progress. On the other hand, one way for displacing a conflict is for the dominant group to move outside of the existing boundaries of struggle. The weakening of spatial boundaries allows new kinds of domination to emerge in both ways. Continuing the example from the workers' movement (introduced above) into the present, one easily recognizes this. The intensification of labour through 'scientific management' was strongly contested during the 1960s, leading to two further displacements: the relocation of industrial production to now so-called emergent economies and the weakening of labour in the North through labour law reforms. The former is a spatial displacement reminiscent of colonialism, but now it implicates free workers elsewhere. The latter undoes the achievements of earlier collective action by widening the competition among workers beyond the boundaries of states.

Thus the erasure of time and space lets new kinds of domination emerge that cannot be characterized as formal domination, but that limit social and political progress and even cause regress in both those respects. The second question, then, is how these new kinds of domination can be criticized and social and political progress reached by overcoming them. As we said before, the force of critique consists in demonstrating that the real is deficient with regard to the possible. With regard to social and political progress, equal freedom for all human beings marked the horizon of the possible, and the absence of equal rights constituted a measure for the distance. But there is no self-evident objective of emancipation any longer once equal legal freedom has been achieved, even though the real may fall far short of the desirable.

This was indeed the reason why the exhaustion of progress was diagnosed during the late twentieth century. But by now our analysis has moved beyond this diagnosis. I have identified new kinds of domination, and have recognized that they were generated by displacements of issues in response to successful resistance to earlier forms of domination. Furthermore, importantly, we have now seen that the erasure of time and space, demanded by an overly abstract concept of individual and collective autonomy, is that which has enabled these new kinds of domination. This leads directly to the conclusion that the reconstitution of historical time and meaningful space marks the line of progress to be pursued in overcoming new kinds of domination. And as my brief analysis above has shown, this is a process that is already going on in different ways in many parts of the globe. It is not an invention based merely on theoretical fiat.

While the direction of this kind of progress is thus clearly marked, it is not as clear how to pursue it. To continue with the example of political progress: as long as participation was denied to categories of persons, thus under conditions of formal political domination, the call for free and equal universal participation rights marked the way of progress. Once equal rights exist, political progress relies on an analysis of the existing kinds of domination that can only be achieved by nuanced interpretation. Are there reasons to assume that some interests regularly prevail over others? Are the conditions for political communication such that all concerns can adequately be raised? Are the forms of participation such that new concerns can be raised by the citizenry such that office holders need to take them into account? Is the balance between individual and collective freedom adequately elaborated? Are political collectivities constituted in such a way that a common will can be formed? And are the political institutions of such a kind that the collective will can be implemented? The interpretation of a situation after the end of formal domination is much more demanding than the one of a situation in which the lack of freedom or equality clearly signalled the goal of progress.

This openness of current situations to interpretation with regard to progress is particularly important exactly because the situations are not free of domination. As we argued above, the struggle against the erasure of space and time is often a reconstitutive movement aiming at progressing towards situations in which social life can be freely organized on the basis of world-interpretations that are created against the background of one's specific experiences and thus provide meaning. But the struggle against the erasure of space and time can also be driven by the power of existing elites who merely resist being dethroned by opposing elites. The erasure of space and time permits displacements that create new kinds of domination. But it also may diminish the power of old elites and thus has a liberating component. Today, we often witness a confusion between the two forms of resistance, resistance against old domination and resistance against new kinds of domination, deliberately enhanced by existing powers. A careful and nuanced analysis of the plurality of ways of interpreting the present is essential for making a distinction between interpretations that are enacting important normative claims and those that use interpretative fragments for their own interests. Progress results from winning the struggle over world-interpretation.

Possible Progress (3): Avoiding Hubris

The same is true for the third kind of progress that is possible and necessary today. We have seen earlier that progress – partial progress, to be sure, predominantly epistemic-economic progress – often occurred through domination. Those who propagated this kind of progress would not speak about domination, but about mastery. The increase of mastery was a key promise of progress from the eighteenth century onwards (chapter 2). It originated in a context in which human beings were very exposed to the vagaries of nature, often unable to secure food supplies or shelter. In the course of the past two centuries, however, human beings have transformed the earth and exploited nature in their pursuit of mastery. Thus doubts have mounted whether the increase of mastery indeed necessarily spells progress, or in different terms, whether that what appeared as increase in mastery is nothing but a temporary phenomenon to be followed by losses of certainty and control that are greater than the perceived gains.

Mastery of nature is today at the centre of concerns about misplaced ambitions of humankind. At a closer look, though, there are two rather similar such phenomena, mastery over nature and mastery over human beings for the supposed benefit of humankind. During the first half of the twentieth century, several gigantic projects of socio-political transformation offered competing visions of the 'new man' and the ways and means to improve humanity. The most well-known of those are Stalinism and Nazism, aiming at a total revolution that would radically transform human beings and their ways of living together. But eugenics, widespread in the

West, differed from totalitarianism in its knowledge base and its acceptance of some degree of liberalism, but not in the objective of improving humankind by intervening at the core, the very nature of the human being itself.

The projects of mastery over nature and mastery over humankind have both aimed at increasing knowledge about their object with a view to using this knowledge for transforming the object in a controlled way, putting it to better use or improving it, bringing it to a higher state, respectively. Both types of projects were strongly criticized after the Second World War, in particular during the 1960s and 1970s, but they have not disappeared. As regards mastery over nature, the first global criticism was the Club of Rome report *Limits to Growth* of 1972, pointing to the depletion of the resources of the earth. Despite widespread concern at the time, by now one can conclude that the predominant reaction to the report has been efforts at discovering more resources and improving techniques of resource extraction, rather than limiting resource consumption. This reaction, in turn, brought about the current situation of threatening irreversible climate change. The intense discussions about the urgent need for lowering emissions signal steps towards a different, non-dominating relation to nature. However, the persistent inability to arrive at a satisfactory global agreement brings a new version of the project of mastering nature onto the agenda. 'Geo-engineering' aims at actively altering the climate of the earth, rather than limiting the ongoing climate-changing activities.

The climate risk should have radically altered the human relation to nature, but it did not. Similarly, the experience of totalitarianism should have led to the abandonment of all radical projects of changing human nature through large-scale social engineering. But this is not the case either. The commitment to 'human rights' apparently leaves the individual human beings freer than ever to pursue their lives.

But competition between human beings for resources and rewards is systematically increased, so that self-realization becomes an obligation to succeed rather than a choice of life-conduct. Societies are no longer seen as containers of solidarity, but as the providers of the frameworks in which enterprising selves can succeed. Rather than eliminating the others directly, as totalitarian domination did with the class enemy and the enemy of the people, the current creation of the 'new men' leaves them behind, as the debris of humankind.

Both these radical projects of transforming nature and of transforming human beings are based on the self-confidence that this can be done, and on the conviction that such transformations will spell progress. They do not consider that similar projects in the past have failed and have led to deterioration rather than progress. The similarity is not recognized because current proponents of radical transformation presume to base their projects on new and higher knowledge. But this was exactly what proponents of the earlier projects did, too. The combination of presumed epistemic superiority, excessive self-confidence and disregard for objections makes such projects hubristic.

Just as the erasure of time and space could not easily be criticized and denounced because it also contained a component of liberation, so the hubristic projects of radical transformation cannot be discarded out of hand because they address existing problems and display a commitment to progress. The strong concept of progress in the past suggested that all change was likely to be progressive: those who were in favour of change were the progressives. The experience with hubristic projects has altered the field of interpretation. Possible and desirable progress now occupies a position between the conservative attitude of always leaving things as they are, on the one hand, and longing hubristically for total revolution, on the other. The precise position cannot be assessed abstractly, but needs to be identified by developing an interpretative judgement of the situation one finds oneself in.

Reversing Recent Regress

Our reconstruction of the experience with progress over the past half century has led to paradoxes. Ever more societies have adopted democratic institutions, but the capacity for collective self-determination has probably decreased. Most forms of formal domination have been overcome, but new kinds of domination have emerged that are more difficult to combat. Epistemic and economic advances continue, but they are often more likely to lead to deterioration rather than to progress, due to the way in which they are applied. Even though progress has not been absent in the recent past, it has been accompanied by regress that often threatens to exceed the benefits of progress.

At the same time, we have recognized that the main 'mechanism' of progress – progress through domination and resistance to domination – that was in force from the late eighteenth century, has ceased to be central during the past half century. It needs to be replaced. This replacement can be found – maybe surprisingly – by a return to the Enlightenment focus on human autonomy. But not by a straight return: we need to be more explicit than the Enlightenment thinkers about the ways in which collective autonomy can emerge from personal autonomy. And we need to abandon the search for theoretical certainty and engage instead in the critical interpretation of the socio-political situation we find ourselves in.

A brief reflection on this situation today has revealed the most significant dangers of regress: that collective 'choices' are more and more determined by the aggregate of numerous individual decisions; that past injustice determines life chances in highly unequal ways behind the veil of equal freedom in the present; that current problems are exacerbated rather than solved through hubris, through ill-conceived instrumental mastery. Confronting these dangers, progress remains both necessary and possible: through building democratic collective agency, overcoming new forms of domination and combating hubris.

Bibliographical Note

This essay draws on numerous sources. To try to list all of them would add an overlong bibliography to a short text, while still running the risk of being unbalanced or too selective. Thus, instead of a full list of references, this note provides bibliographical information about key sources of inspiration and about the approach developed, including that in my own earlier work which offers more detailed references.

In addition, full references are provided chapter by chapter only to those sources that are cited verbatim or for very specific matter. Canonical writings, which today can easily be found on the internet, even in full-text versions – such as works by Rousseau or Kant referred to in chapter 1 or by Marx or Weber in chapter 4 – are not listed. For the same reason, more recent works that are widely cited for particular expressions or insights – such as the writings of Lyotard, Fukuyama and Rorty referred to in chapter 1, W. B. Gallie's 'essentially contested concepts' or Walt Rostow's 'take-off' – are also excluded.

The Approach

This essay is a work in conceptually guided historical sociology linked to debates about agency, interpretation and structure in social theory, as well as about freedom and domination in political philosophy. The main contours of the approach have been presented in my *Modernity as Experience and Interpretation* (Cambridge: Polity, 2008), chapters 13 and 14. My first attempt in this direction had been *A Sociology of Modernity: Liberty and Discipline* (London: Routledge, 1994), a work that gives much more historical detail, but employs only very general conceptual ideas and is limited to a study of Western Europe and brief glimpses at the experiences of the United States of America and of East European Soviet-style socialism.

Among the classical authors, the main sources of inspiration are Karl Marx's writings, provided that *Capital* and the political writings are read together, Alexis de Tocqueville's *Democracy in America* and *The Old Regime and the French Revolution*, and Max Weber's *Protestant Ethic and the 'Spirit' of Capitalism*. While these works inaugurate a certain kind of historical sociology, aiming to understand social phenomena of large scale and long duration and posing questions about the dynamics of social change, they are shaped by expectations of progress prevalent during the nineteenth century. Karl Polanyi's *Great Transformation* and Hannah Arendt's *Origins of Totalitarianism* demonstrate by mid-twentieth century the fragility of nineteenth-century socio-political innovations.

During the closing decades of the twentieth century, this kind of historical sociology was on the verge of being abandoned. The approach was troubled by theoretical and methodological doubts about the possibility of analysing large-scale phenomena and their dynamics of transformation, as well as by politico-historical doubts, which culminated in the decline of the belief in a progressive logic of history that is at the centre of this essay. Today one cannot – or at least should not – write about long stretches of history without taking these doubts into account. This means that one has to reassemble historical sociology by reviving the old questions but trying to answer them by more adequate means. Among the components that achieve this greater adequacy are the following.

From the 1960s onwards, social transformations came to be explicitly seen in the light of conceptual transformations. The approach that has been found most useful for this essay is the historiography of concepts as pioneered by Reinhart Koselleck: see in particular his *Futures Past: On the Semantics of Historical Time* (New York: Columbia University Press, 2004 [1979]), but it needs to be read in conjunction with Michel Foucault's archaeology and geneaology of discourses and Quentin Skinner's renewal of the history of political thought (see chapter 13 of my *Modernity as Experience and Interpretation*).

'Modernity' has a central place among the concepts to be reconsidered. Even though the term was little used as a noun before the 1980s, the idea of present socio-political organization being marked by a radical rupture with the past – which gave rise to the strong concept of progress, as discussed in chapter 1 – informed much political thought from the late eighteenth century onwards, as well as the emerging social sciences during the nineteenth century. A most explicit example is Benjamin Constant's speech 'De la liberté des anciens comparée avec celle des modernes' of 1819. From Tocqueville and Marx at mid-nineteenth century to Talcott Parsons and Jürgen Habermas more than a century later, there was little doubt about the existence of this rupture and its key significance for 'modern societies'. This entire tradition of thought was marked by its emphasis on new institutions – capitalism/markets, bureaucracy, democracy – and by a polarized attitude to the new society, either embracing it as realizing the normative promises of the Enlightenment or criticizing it for betraying or even undermining these promises. Only in recent debates has it been recognized that the institutional emphasis underestimates the importance of experiences of modernity and that the polarization between affirmative and critical approaches narrows down the variety of interpretations of modernity. In *Theorizing Modernity* (London: Sage, 2001), *Modernity as Experience and Interpretation* and *Modernity: Understanding the Present* (Cambridge: Polity, 2012), I have tried to elaborate a different understanding of modernity, drawing significantly on Cornelius Castoriadis's work in *L'institution imaginaire de la société* (Paris: Seuil, 1975) and various writings published in *Les carrefours du labyrinthe* (Paris: Seuil, various years), in particular on 'autonomy', as well as on Johann P. Arnason's social philosophy and historical-comparative sociology. For the latter, I would like to single out the essays on 'The imaginary constitution of modernity', *Revue Européenne des Sciences Sociales*, 1989, pp. 323–37; 'Modernity as project and as field of tensions', in Axel Honneth and Hans Joas (eds), *Communicative Action* (Cambridge: Polity, 1991); 'World interpretations and mutual understanding', in Axel Honneth et al. (eds), *Cultural-Political Interventions in the Unfinished Project of Enlightenment* (Cambridge, MA: MIT Press, 1992); and the magisterial *Civilizations in Dispute: Historical Questions and Theoretical Traditions* (Leiden: Brill, 2003).

Such rethinking of 'modernity' in the light of the history of the past two centuries entails a reconsideration of the relation between the social sciences, on the one hand, and the societies and polities that are being investigated, on the other, and in particular of the relation between normative claims and empirical realities. Reinhart Koselleck's historical reflections on 'critique and crisis' stand in the background of such reconsideration, which has more recently given rise to two impressive research programmes, the one pursued in the 'sociology of critical capacity', launched by Luc Boltanski and Laurent Thévenot (see, in particular, *De la Justification*, Paris: Gallimard, 1991, by both authors; and *De la Critique*, Paris: Gallimard, 2009, by Boltanski), and the other by Axel Honneth and his colleagues at the Institute for Social Research in Frankfurt (see Martin Hartmann and Axel Honneth, 'Paradoxes of capitalism', *Constellations* 13(1) (2006): 41–58; Axel Honneth and Ferdinand Sutterlüty, 'Normative Paradoxien der Gegenwart', *Westend. Neue Zeitschrift für Sozialforschung* 8(1) (2011): 67–85). These approaches have in common that they consider normative claims as empirical phenomena. Thus, rather than being part of a separate genre of (political) philosophy, the analysis of such claims becomes an integral part of the investigation of social phenomena – and of social change in particular. In this context, I should also mention the work by William H. Sewell Jr, starting out from the analysis of changes in political language in post-revolutionary France (*Work and Revolution in France: The Language of Labor from the Old Regime to 1848*, Cambridge: Cambridge University Press, 1980) and culminating in the most coherent attempt in bringing together insights from social theory and historical sociology towards a new understanding of social transformations (*Logics of History: Social Theory and Social Transformation*, Chicago: University of Chicago Press, 2005).

Considering the sum of the above-mentioned works, many conceptual and historical elements are in place for the re-elaboration of historical sociology, but an adequately developed global perspective is still sorely missing, as has been made clear by recent 'southern theory and history', as well as by global history. Key works are: Dipesh Chakrabarty, *Provincializing Europe: Postcolonial Thought and*

Historical Difference (Princeton: Princeton University Press, 2000); Achille Mbembe, *On the Postcolony* (Berkeley: University of California Press, 2001); Enrique Dussel, *Politics of Liberation: A Critical Global History* (Norwich: SCM Press, 2011 [2007]); Jürgen Osterhammel, *The Transformation of the World: A Global History of the Nineteenth Century* (Princeton: Princeton University Press, 2014 [2009]). In some such works, importantly, the connection between economic history and the analysis of major transformations has recently been revived, such as in Kenneth Pomeranz, *The Great Divergence: China, Europe, and the Making of the Modern World-Economy* (Princeton: Princeton University Press, 2000); and Bo Stråth, *Three Utopias of Peace and the Search for a Political Economy* (London: Bloomsbury, forthcoming).

Insights from these sources have entered into the comparative-historical research and work at conceptual retrieval, pursued within the framework of the research project *Trajectories of Modernity: Comparing Non-European and European Varieties*, funded by the European Research Council as Advanced Grant no. 249438 from 2010 to 2015, which, in turn, has provided the backdrop to this essay. Key results from this project have been published, or are in preparation, as: Peter Wagner (ed.), *African, American and European Trajectories of Modernity: Past Oppression, Future Justice?*, vol. 2 of the *Annual of European and Global Studies* (Edinburgh: Edinburgh University Press, 2015); Gerard Rosich and Peter Wagner (eds), *The Trouble with Democracy: Political Modernity in the 21st Century* (Edinburgh: Edinburgh University Press, 2015); 'Modernity and capitalism', ed. by David Casassas and Peter Wagner, special issue of the *European Journal of Social Theory* 19(2) (2016); and Jacob Dlamini, Aurea Mota, Peter Wagner, *Possible Futures: Trajectories of Modernity in Brazil, South Africa and Europe*, in preparation. The analysis of the recent social transformation, explored above in chapters 5 and 6, is sketched in some more detail in: Peter Wagner, 'Interpreting the present: a research programme', *Social Imaginaries* 1(1) (2015).

Ultimately, indeed, the aim of this conceptually guided historical sociology is to provide a diagnosis of the present that can help us to situate ourselves in our own time. In this regard, this essay, short as it is, is in communication with such monumental attempts as Jeffrey C. Alexander's recent *The Civil Sphere* (Oxford: Oxford University Press, 2006), Michael Mann's tetralogy on *The Sources of Social Power*, of which volumes 3 and 4 have just been published (Cambridge: Cambridge University Press, 2012 and 2013), and, as concerns the analysis of the political *problématique*, the works by Pierre Rosanvallon (most recently *La Société des égaux*, Paris: Seuil, 2011) and Marcel Gauchet (for instance, the trilogy on *L'Avènement de la démocratie*, Paris: Gallimard, 2007–2010). How the perspectives differ may be left for future discussion.

Additional References

Foreword

Fabian, Johannes, 1983, *Time and the Other*. New York: Columbia University Press.

Mota, Aurea, 2015, 'The American divergence, the modern western world, and the *paradigmatisation* of history', in Peter Wagner (ed.), *African, American and European Trajectories of Modernity: Annual of European and Global Studies*, vol. 2. Edinburgh: Edinburgh University Press.

Chapter 1 The Withering Away of Progress

Habermas, Jürgen, 1990, *Die nachholende Revolution. Kleine politische Schriften, vol. VII*. Frankfurt/M: Suhrkamp.

Hall, Peter A. and Lamont, Michèle (eds), 2009, *Successful Societies: How Institutions and Culture Affect Health*. Cambridge: Cambridge University Press.

Koselleck, Reinhart, 2006, *Begriffsgeschichten*. Frankfurt/M: Suhrkamp.

Koselleck, Reinhart and Reichardt, Rolf (eds), 1988, *Die Französische Revolution als Bruch des gesellschaftlichen Bewusstseins*. Munich: Oldenbourg.

Offe, Claus, 2010, 'Was (falls überhaupt etwas) können wir uns heute unter politischem Fortschritt vorstellen?', *Westend. Neue Zeitschrift für Sozialforschung* 7(2): 3–14.

Rorty, Richard, 1989, *Contingency, Irony, Solidarity*. Cambridge: Cambridge University Press, p. 63.

Chapter 2   Progress as Mechanism: The Epistemic-Economic Complex

Berman, Marshall, 1982, *All That is Solid Melts into Air: The Experience of Modernity*. New York: Simon and Schuster.

Boltanski, Luc and Chiapello, Eve, 1999, *Le nouvel esprit du capitalisme*. Paris: Gallimard.

Chakrabarty, Dipesh, 2009, 'The climate of history: four theses', *Critical Inquiry* 35: 197–222.

Fraisse, Robert, 1981, 'Les sciences sociales: utilisation, dépendance, autonomie', *Sociologie du Travail* 23(4): 369–83.

Hauff, Volker and Scharpf, Fritz W., 1975, *Modernisierung der Volkswirtschaft*. Cologne: EVA.

Maddison, Angus, 1982, *Phases of Capitalist Development*. Oxford: Oxford University Press.

Maddison, Angus, 2007, *Contours of the World Economy, 1–2030 AD: Essays in Macro-Economic History*. Oxford: Oxford University Press.

O'Brien, Patrick, 2010, 'Ten years of debate on the origins of the Great Divergence', *Reviews in History*, http://www.history.ac.uk/reviews/review/1008; accessed on 4 January 2015.

Piketty, Thomas, 2013, *Le Capital au 21e siècle*. Paris: Seuil.

Pomeranz, Kenneth, 2000, *The Great Divergence: China, Europe, and the Making of the Modern World-Economy*. Princeton: Princeton University Press.

Schivelbusch, Wolfgang, 1977, *Geschichte der Eisenbahnreise. Zur Industrialisierung von Raum und Zeit im 19. Jahrhundert.* Munich: Hanser.

Wittrock, Björn, 1985, 'Dinosaurs or dolphins? Rise and resurgence of the research-oriented university', in Björn Wittrock and Aant Elzinga (eds), *The University Research System*. Stockholm: Almqvist and Wiksell.

Chapter 3   Progress as Struggle under Conditions of Ambivalence

Fuster Peiró, Lorena Angela and Rosich, Gerard, 2015, 'The limits of recognition: history, otherness, autonomy', in Peter Wagner (ed.), *African, American and European Trajectories of Modernity, Annual of European and Global Studies*, vol. 2. Edinburgh: Edinburgh University Press.

Honneth, Axel, 2004, 'Organized self-realization: Some paradoxes of individualization', *European Journal of Social Theory* 7(4): 463–78.

Karagiannis, Nathalie, 2004, *Avoiding Responsibility: The Politics and Discourse of EU Development Policy*. London: Pluto.

Karagiannis, Nathalie and Wagner, Peter, 2013, 'The liberty of the moderns compared to the liberty of the ancients', in Johann P. Arnason, Kurt Raaflaub and Peter Wagner (eds), *The Greek Polis and the Invention of Democracy: A Politico-Cultural Transformation and its Interpretations*. Oxford: Blackwell.

Noiriel, Gérard, 1991, *La tyrannie du national: le droit d'asyle en Europe (1793–1993)*. Paris: Calmann-Lévy.

Pagden, Anthony (ed.), 2000, *Facing Each Other. Europe's Perception of the World and the World's Perception of Europe*. London: Ashgate.

Taylor, Charles, 1989, *Sources of the Self*. Cambridge, MA: Belknap Press of Harvard University Press.

Chapter 4   The Idea of Progress Revisited

Baker, Keith Michael, 1990, *Inventing the French Revolution*. Cambridge: Cambridge University Press.

Burke, Edmund, 1993 (1790), *Reflections on the Revolution in France*. Oxford: Oxford University Press.

Eisenstadt, Shmuel N., 2000, 'Multiple modernities', *Daedalus* (Winter): 1–29.

Groh, Dieter, 1973, *Negative Integration und revolutionärer Attentismus*. Frankfurt/M: Propyläen.

Habermas, Jürgen, 1962, *Strukturwandel der Öffentlichkeit*. Neuwied: Luchterhand.

Halperin, Sandra, 2004, *War and Social Change in Modern Europe: The Great Transformation Revisited*. Cambridge: Cambridge University Press.

Hirschman, Albert, 1991, *The Rhetoric of Reaction: Perversity, Futility, Jeopardy*. Cambridge, MA: Belknap Press of Harvard University Press.

Karagiannis, Nathalie and Wagner, Peter, 2008, 'Varieties of agonism: conflict, the common good and the need for synagonism', *Journal of Social Philosophy* 39(3): 323–39.

Latour, Bruno, 1991, *Nous n'avons jamais été modernes*. Paris: La Découverte.

Luxemburg, Rosa, 2000 (1916), *Die Krise der Sozialdemokratie (Die 'Junius'-Broschüre)*, in *Gesammelte Werke*, vol. 4 (sixth revised edn). Berlin: Dietz, pp. 51–164.

Stein, Lorenz von, 1850, *Die Geschichte der sozialen Bewegung in Frankreich von 1789 bis auf unsere Tage*. Leipzig: Wigand.

Chapter 5 The Past Half Century

Benjamin, Walter, 1969, *Illuminations*. New York: Schocken.

Foucault, Michel, 1984, 'What is Enlightenment?', in Paul Rabinow (ed.), *The Foucault Reader*. New York: Pantheon Books.

Fourastié, Jean, 1979, *Les Trente Glorieuses, ou la révolution invisible de 1946 à 1975*. Paris: Fayard.

Jaspers, Karl, 1968 (1949), *The Origin and Goal of History*. New Haven: Yale University Press.

Parsons, Talcott, 1971, *The System of Modern Societies*. Englewood Cliffs, NJ: Prentice-Hall.

Rawls, John, 1971, *A Theory of Justice*. Cambridge, MA: Belknap Press of Harvard University Press.

Chapter 6 Possible Progress Today

Gaonkar, Dilip Parameshwar (ed.), 2001, *Alternative Modernities*. Durham, NC: Duke University Press.

Gerschenkron, Alexander, 1962, *Economic Backwardness in Historical Perspective*. Cambridge, MA: Harvard University Press.

Nedimović, Svjetlana, 2015, 'An unsettled past as a political resource', in Peter Wagner (ed.), *African, American and European Trajectories of Modernity, Annual of European and Global Studies*, vol. 2. Edinburgh: Edinburgh University Press.

Streeck, Wolfgang, 2011, 'The crisis of democratic capitalism', *New Left Review* 71: 5–29.

Index